TRUTH IS THE ARROW, MERCY IS THE BOW

A DIY MANUAL FOR THE CONSTRUCTION OF STORIES

STEVE ALMOND

TRUTH IS THE ARROW, MERCY IS THE BOW

A DIY Manual for the Construction of Stories

NEW YORK

zandoprojects.com

First Edition: April 2024

Text design by Aubrey Khan, Neuwirth & Associates, Inc.
"Free Write" pencil by Alex Muravev from Noun Project
Cover design by Evan Gaffney
Cover pencil isolated © vitalyzorkin | Adobe Stock

The publisher does not have control over and is not responsible for author or other third-party websites (or their content).

Library of Congress Control Number: 2023946074

978-1-63893-130-0 (Paperback)
978-1-63893-131-7 (ebook)

10 9 8 7 6 5 4 3 2
Manufactured in the United States of America

For Richard Almond

Blunt dad, soul doctor, truth seeker

At the bottom of the ocean you might find a pearl

Don't let your heart get broken by this world

—DAN BERN

CONTENTS

CONTENTS

PART II.
SOURCE MATERIALS

PART III.
MEDITATIONS

CONTENTS

PART IV.

TRUTH IS THE ARROW, MERCY IS THE BOW

A DIY MANUAL FOR THE CONSTRUCTION OF STORIES

BY WAY OF HELLO

RED BICYCLE, WHITE MOON

In May of 2019, by some colossal blunder of optimism and mistaken identity, I was invited to deliver the keynote address at the Boao International Forum on Writing Education. What did this mean? Who was Boao? I had no idea.

Six weeks later, I stood in an immense outdoor mall on the outskirts of Beijing. It was nearing dusk. The concrete paths glowed orange. I was handed a microphone and told to address a cadre of dignitaries, which apparently I did, then shown an array of pastel booths celebrating the wonders of writing. Shoppers gawked, in poignant confusion, then swooped into the brightly lit showrooms of American Eagle and Victoria's Secret.

The keynote was held in a movie theater. Promotional posters hung all around, identifying me, fervently and erroneously, as a *Famous Harvard Professor*. Before I could take the stage, a government official seized my passport, at which he squinted for some minutes, while my chaperones circled in a panic.

Eventually, I was permitted to deliver my address. It was greeted with widespread bafflement. My translator Shiro (he was, confusingly, Japanese) later explained: the speech centered on a tale of sibling rivalry; owing to China's one-child policy, almost no one in attendance had any siblings.

Having botched my central commission, I looked forward to retiring to my hotel room for a nourishing bout of self-hatred. I was delivered instead to a dismal flat on the twenty-first floor of a condo tower. My cell phone didn't work and there was no internet, so presumably I would be able to sleep, but my circadian functions were frayed from a sixteen-hour flight over the polar icecap. At some point, I did lose consciousness, which I only know because I was jolted awake minutes later by a home alarm on the scale of Wagner, accompanied by a robotic voice imprecating me in Mandarin.

I staggered about in the dark, introducing my face to various inconveniently placed walls before locating the control panel, a flashing red square decorated with frightening symbols. I pawed at these for a time, envisioning the scene that would ensue once the police arrived. My hosts had taken possession of my passport, naturally, which meant my only source of identification was a mangled copy of the previously cited promotional poster. *Famous Harvard Professor Detained*, the headlines would read. *American University Denies Affiliation with Incoherent Fugitive.*

The Forum was going perhaps worse than expected.

Organizers described my final duty as a "live demonstration." I assumed this meant teaching a few ringers at a local university. Instead, I was led to the cavernous banquet room of a bustling restaurant, which smelled, deliciously, of garlic.

It was crammed with teachers, many of whom had flown thousands of miles to see me, all of whom were poised to set pen to notebook. Shiro explained that China had little formal tradition when it came to creative writing training. I would now show three hundred instructors—and by extension, in my own grandiose vision, *the entire country*—how to teach creative writing.

Presently, my pupils appeared: a procession of uniformed seventh graders from a local private school. They filed into seats at the front of the room, looking as miserable as you might expect, which is to say slightly less miserable than me.

One of the unexpected benefits of operating on an hour of sleep, in a country far from home, is that, at a certain point, you surrender the notion that you will be of use to anyone. I had reached that point. And so I launched into a sermon about the literary dividends of obsession—you'll encounter a version seventy or so pages down the road—ardently seeking eye contact with my charges, who were, understandably, staring at Shiro, the dashing translator. I then asked them to write about an obsession from early childhood. In America, the protocol was pretty straightforward. Here, it would involve five additional steps:

* Shiro translates my instructions into Mandarin

* The students write, then read, their pieces in Mandarin

* Shiro translates them into English for me

* I offer feedback in English

* Which Shiro translates back into Mandarin

How would all this go? My money was on disaster. The students looked solemn, dutiful, petrified. They were, it seemed to me, trapped in a kind of anxiety fugue, which, years from now, they would attempt to describe to some patient lover.

Yes, that was the day I was plucked from my normal class and put on a bus. I believe it was a punishment of some kind. They drove me to a vast cafeteria filled with hundreds of teachers. Some creepy American man began raving. They said he was the teacher but he dressed like a vagrant. He ordered me to write a personal story, which I had to recite while the strange teacher stared at me . . .

I probably don't need to tell you that not one student volunteered to read. Nor that a sense of doom descended upon that room. But then the plot took an unexpected turn. A slender girl rose from her seat and, trembling only slightly, read a stunning piece of prose.

It was about the bicycle she had coveted as a child, a gleaming red machine with silver handlebars and tassels. She spied it in the main square of her town, resting against a fountain. Her father felt a bike would be a distraction from her studies, and her mother didn't argue with her father. In dreams, the bike shone under the white moon. She imagined riding it constantly. She could feel her legs pumping. When she closed her eyes, it was still there, under the moon, slightly too large for her, incandescent. Once, when no one was around, she rode the red bicycle. Or maybe she made that part up. It felt like flying. She rode it all the way to the next town, then to the moon. She never came back.

Shiro whispered his translation. It was urgent and dizzying. The girl's voice rang out like a hymn. When she had finished, there was a sustained silence, as if we were in church.

Suddenly, a figure in back—one of the few male teachers in the room—jumped to his feet and began yelling. Shiro provided a play-by-play of his rant: He didn't understand what sort of class this was, or how such an assignment would be graded. What criteria could be applied to such a text? It was all just romantic nonsense. His face flushed.

But he was immediately enveloped by a sea of women who were no less furious. They began to yell at him to quiet down. For a few glorious moments, it appeared they might wrestle him to the ground. Apparently, they had endured men like this before.

I don't remember what sort of notes I offered the girl. It hardly matters. We'd all felt the same holy jolt. I've gone looking for that feeling everywhere. From time to time, I've found it in my own writing. More often, it happens in the classroom. Even in China, amid the blaring alarms and briars of translation.

I happen to believe that every single person on earth is a storyteller. We are all trying to understand the story of our lives. Some of us are also trying to make a career, or a calling, from the practice of writing. The essential tools of that pursuit are patience and forgiveness and courage. You have to want to tell the truth.

The essays collected here are a compendium of insights and anecdotes drawn from my struggles as a writer, and my work as a teacher. There's a section on craft, a section on the origins of story, a section that reckons with the psychic and emotional barriers we face in our ambivalent pursuit of truth.

It can be tempting to retreat into the technical, or the mystical, when it comes to writing. For the most part, you sit alone and make decisions. You reach inward, toward the joys and sorrows you are meant to share with the world. Toward the red bicycle beneath a white moon. I hope this book will be a worthy accomplice.

STEVE ALMOND
Arlington, MA
July 2023

PART I

DEMYSTIFYING
THE CRAFT

ARRANGING INCIDENTS

HOW TO MAKE PLOT YOUR FRIEND

To start at the beginning: I suck at plot. More broadly, I suck at planning. I am not an organized person.

The office in which I am composing this confessional stands as evidence. The filing cabinet beside me, which is supposed to be a place where important documents are *filed*, is instead stuffed with the items that accumulate on the flat surfaces of my office (mostly the floor) and which might include, at any given moment, such as the present one, an array of bled-out pens, snarled headphone cords, a fluorescent orange parking ticket from the City of Fuck You Boston, a talking key chain from the 1980s teen rom-com *Sixteen Candles*, and a half-eaten Ghirardelli chocolate bar. OK, three-quarters eaten.

For most of my life as a writer, I've gotten away with sucking at plot. I started out as a journalist, so my assignments provided the plot. When I moved to short stories, I did so with an intuitive sense of plot—that it had something to do with building a ramp to moments of high drama, then slowing down. It took me a decade or so, but I got the hang of stories.

Novels, on the other hand.

Novels I have failed at chronically. And for reasons that are now quite discernible to me. My five unpublished manuscripts (which, were I more organized, would be stored in my file cabinet) share the same essential flaw—a meandering plot. They contained a multitude of set pieces and precious little rising action.

Plot is the most intricate, and therefore elusive, aspect of storytelling: sustaining forward momentum over the long haul. The architecture of a novel, in particular, requires the creation of stakes for all your major characters, as well as intersecting (and interdependent) trajectories. You can ride style and voice for fifty to a hundred pages. After that, you need a blueprint.

Weirdly, it was Aristotle who helped me grasp this.

To provide the proper context: I had just finished a draft of my fifth novel. The book was an attempt to reverse the pattern of my previous novels, which had been burdened by passive protagonists. *Bucky Dunn Is Running* was about a hedonistic demagogue who runs for president. How could this garish pursuit of acclaim not rank as plot? And yet, I had a sinking feeling in my gut, which was eventually confirmed by various editors. The novel had plenty of velocity but not much direction.

This is where the *Poetics* entered the story. In the midst of preparing for a class, in my not very organized way, I stumbled across this:

But most important of all is the **structure of the incidents**. For Tragedy is an imitation, not of men, but of an action and of life, and life consists in action, and its end is a mode of action, not a quality. Now character determines men's qualities, but it is by their actions that they are happy or the reverse ... If you string together a set of speeches expressive of character, and well finished in point of diction and thought, you will not produce the essential tragic effect nearly so well as with a play which, however deficient in these respects, yet has a plot and artistically constructed incidents.

It was not enough for me to "string together a set of speeches" for Bucky to deliver. My hero needed to act in ways that changed his fortune. Aristotle (that asshole) was even more explicit. This change, he observed, should be accompanied "by Reversal, or by Recognition, or by both. These last should arise from the internal structure of the plot, so that what follows should be the necessary or probable result of the preceding action."

Plot, in other words, resides in establishing a clear chain of consequence. Not this happens *and* this happens *and* this happens. But: this happens, *therefore* that happens. And *because* that happened, this next thing happens. My scenes needed to expose hidden truths (Recognition), upend expectations (Reversal), escalate tension, and instigate further action.

When I reexamined the scenes in my previous novels, I could see that they were hardly ever achieving these goals. More often, they were protecting my characters from the dangers of Recognition and Reversal, indulging their blind spots rather than exposing them.

As I thought more deeply about this pattern, I realized that early in the drafting process, I wasn't thinking about plot at all.

I was simply trying to get a beat on my characters, who they were and what they wanted. Thus, I spent a lot of time simply marching them around their daily routines and hoping they would bump into plot.

I should have been, but wasn't, asking certain fundamental questions, such as: What possible fates await my heroine? What obstacles stand in her way? By what actions might she find love or ruin? Redemption or damnation?

This kind of thinking requires the author to step back and consider the larger arc of her story. And again, speaking bluntly, I suck at this kind of stepping back. I'm an inveterate improviser. Put more precisely: I use scenes to *conceive* of plot rather than to *dramatize* and *advance* plot.

This methodology, I'm unhappy to report, has proved spectacularly inefficient. When I don't know where a story is headed, I flog the language. It's a kind of anxious literary vamping. By contrast, when I know where a story is headed, I instantly relax and focus my attention on the task at hand: writing the next scene dictated by the chain of consequence.

If you're confused about which scenes belong in your story, start by asking the elemental question: What *work* is this scene doing? Is there Recognition? Is there Reversal? Are you introducing or escalating conflict? Instigating subsequent action? That may sound like a tough ask. But expecting a reader to muddle through a bunch of scenes until you figure out the story you want to tell is an even tougher order.

I MISLED YOU A FEW PARAGRAPHS BACK. That's bound to happen in a book like this, written by a neurotic striving to sound sure of himself. I'm bound to write sentences that over-simplify my experience. Such as this: *It took me a decade or so, but I got the hang of short stories.* The truth is more like: because of my quick and distracted mind, and my aversion to risk, I feel more comfortable writing stories, where the consequences of failure aren't quite so dire.

I've learned to recognize and manage plot on a smaller scale. Some years ago, for instance, while lying on my analyst's well-funded couch, I began to think about his view of things, specifically the fact that he could see the cuffs of my ears. If I felt shame, my analyst would know, because these cuffs would turn red.

I began to wonder what this might mean in the context of poker, where players are always looking for involuntary signs, or *tells*, that their opponents are bluffing. This no doubt has to do with the fact that I play poker, and that my psychoanalyst father plays even more seriously. But it's the force of my curiosity that matters here, not the source. What generates story is a chain of associations cleaved to a chain of consequence.

And thus, lying on that couch, I began to envision a story about a nebbishy psychoanalyst who is secretly addicted to poker. To his patients, he is a model of compassion and equa-nimity. At the poker table, he's a psychopath. In initial versions, the story ended with his wife catching him. But I kept asking myself: What would up the ante here? What would flush this guy's shadow self out into the open?

I began to climb the chain of consequence. What if the shrink's wife catches him at the *beginning* of the story, and forces him to stop playing? What if the world's greatest poker player then walks into his office, seeking treatment? What if the good doctor is lured back to the poker table by this troubled soul? What if he arrives with a secret bit of knowledge: that his patient's ears turn red when he's bluffing?

I'm not suggesting this story *wrote itself*; that idea is complete horseshit. I'm saying that stories are easier to write—more organic, less labored—when you know where your plot is headed, when the rising action leads, inexorably, to a high-stakes showdown.

A FEW YEARS BACK, I taught a class on my favorite novel, *Stoner*, by John Williams. I analyzed every scene in the book, asking that simple question: What work does it do? I was most astonished by an unassuming passage in which our hero, William Stoner, is teaching the first session of a graduate workshop on medieval literature.

As the scene opens, Stoner is easing into the subject. His enthrallment with literature helps him overcome his crippling self-consciousness (reversal #1) and reveals his hidden talents as a teacher (recognition #1). But his momentum is broken by a brash, disabled student named Walker, who bustles into class late and asks obnoxious questions (reversal #2). Stoner is furious but unable to confront Walker because of his aversion to conflict (recognition #2). Walker is the protégé of a powerful colleague who will become Stoner's lifelong rival. Thus, the scene instigates and escalates a budding rivalry. If that was all this scene did, well, dayenu—*it would have been enough*. But it also introduces us to another student in the class, Katherine, who will become Stoner's mistress. We get all this in two pages.

Because the author has a clear conception of the novel's chain of consequence, the scene plants multiple depth charges, moments whose full impact will detonate only later, when we discover how Walker is setting up Stoner, or come to recognize the awkwardness of his initial encounter with Katherine as erotic confusion.

I think here of another unexpectedly devastating scene, this one from the wonderful novel *The Last Chicken in America* by Ellen Litman. (Full disclosure: Ellen was one of my first writing students!)

Our narrator, nineteen-year-old Masha, has recently immigrated from Moscow to Pittsburgh with her parents. As they depart a remedial English class, their teacher calls out, "See you later, alligator." Masha's mother doesn't understand and asks, in Russian, what the teacher said. Her father refuses to explain.

"Then there are tears," Masha reports. "Right in the middle of the street my mother is crying. Her lips twist helplessly and her face bunches up." She believes her husband and daughter are hiding things from her, that they're ashamed of her poor English.

In 250 words, Litman engineers an astonishing reversal. Stripped of language and dignity, this trio of striving immigrants is revealed as a family in crisis. Their darkest selves emerge, leaving Masha trapped between a cruel, impatient father and a delicate, histrionic mother. "I hate being in the middle," she declares. "I hate being with them at all times, everywhere they go—classes, welfare, dentist's office, supermarket. I translate forms and letters; I interpret. This is my job and I'm required to go along."

This tiny moment is among the most potent portrayals of immigration I've ever read. Because Litman has dramatized the particular slice of life where her characters' primal emotions explode into view.

Writers of nonfiction must also be willing to write what a teacher of mine once dubbed The Obligatory Emotional Scene. The best example I can offer comes from Grace Talusan's *The Body Papers*. This memoir plumbs a range of volatile subjects: racism, sexual abuse, generational trauma. At its center is Talusan's aching desire to bear a child, which she must weigh against the threat of ovarian cancer.

After a battery of tests and consultations, she decides to undergo IVF, before having her ovaries removed. On the day she is set to begin, her doctor warns her and her husband, Alonso, that the process will be grueling. He wants to make sure they're both on board.

"I bounced nervously on my chair, smiling, and then I looked at my husband," Talusan writes. "He didn't have to say a word. I studied his face for only a moment and then started to weep, loudly. I saw in his expression the look of someone who would do anything for me, including having a child that he did not want."

The recognition of Alonso's true feelings constitutes a hairpin reversal—from joy to despondence in half a second. Yet Talusan refuses to rush through the pain. She envisions her marital life spinning out "in a flash," how Alonso would carry out his paternal duties, but "without joy. This would be the end of us."

Rather than playing to the balconies, the prose is measured, which forces readers to bear the emotion of the scene. "I understood then that motherhood was over for me," Talusan reflects. "I could not subject my husband to this relationship that he did not fully want. And I would not sentence our child, who I imagined I loved already, to a father who was so uncertain."

In studying scenes like this, I divined the ultimate point at which Aristotle was driving. Plot shouldn't just spur external action. It should expose the internal conflicts that plague your characters. Having finally grasped this, I came to my sixth novel better prepared.

My protagonist, Lorena, was a fiercely intelligent teenage girl who had been told all her life to remain invisible, because her family was undocumented. Yet she ached to be seen, recognized, desired. I was able to activate this conflict simply by allowing her to visit the home of a rich classmate, where she becomes visible in ways that are both enthralling and dangerous. Blind to the predatory nature of the adults around her, Lorena acts on her yearnings in ways that lead to the wrongful arrest of her brother.

Because of my aversion to planning, I did not have an elaborate sense of plot, just a set of vital intuitions. I knew, for instance, that Lorena would seek to exonerate her brother, and that she would have to summon all her courage and cunning to recruit an unexpected ally: the officer who arrested him. I knew they would wind up in the desert together, scouring the sand for evidence, and that this cop would become, however reluctantly, a father figure. I could see them in my mind, huddled under the stars.

As Lorena set about expanding her world, I recognized it as my duty to understand all the characters whose actions played a role in her fate, especially those who acted destructively. This required me to suspend judgment and instead ponder the secrets they were bearing. For the first time in my miserable career as a would-be novelist, I experienced the sheer, propulsive power of plot as the pursuit of revelation.

After years of pushing, I finally felt pulled through a story by an energetic curiosity, one that radiated outward from Lorena and came to include everyone in her orbit. The novel sprawled, but my job became more focused. I had to write those scenes—and only those scenes—that impelled my characters, tenderly and ruthlessly, toward the truth of themselves.

MAKE THEM ROUND, MAKE THEM DEEP

NOTES ON CHARACTER

I can't remember where I heard this, but here's a story I tell my students about characterization:

Joseph Conrad is having lunch with friends in a Paris cafe when in walks a stunning woman. Actually, let's make it a man: tall, broad-shouldered, tailored suit, face of a Grecian statue. Everyone is transfixed. As he saunters across the room, one of Conrad's pals leans over and says, "Hey, Conrad, you're the famous writer in this probably apocryphal story. What's the one detail you would include, if you wrote about that fellow?" Conrad studies the man for a few seconds, then murmurs, "He has a speck of dirt on the inner rim of his right nostril." I love what this story suggests about writers paying more careful attention to the people around them, looking beyond the obvious signifiers. And yet . . .

How much can we really know about someone based on nostril hygiene alone?

In my own struggles with characterization, the snag is nearly always insufficient data. My construction of character, at least in initial drafts, is often just a description. I provide a facial feature or two, a profession, maybe a verbal tic. I think, *OK, that should be enough*. It's not enough.

Because every person around us—from the bored bureaucrat putting us on hold to the tool who just flipped us off in traffic—possesses a rich and tortured inner life. The feeling we get when we read a great story is that we've come to know the protagonist as deeply as we know our own beloveds. How do we, as writers, perform that feat?

BEFORE WE DIVE INTO THE DEEP END, let's acknowledge that we do not have to plumb the depths of everyone who might appear in our stories.

As E. M. Forster reminds us, in *Aspects of the Novel*, certain characters are intentionally one-dimensional. Still others serve a functional role in our stories. But the characters we are meant to care about must be round: complex, contradictory, capable of evolving, and thus surprising the reader in a convincing way.

This standard applies not just to our heroine, but to the coterie of major characters whose duty it is to confront, tempt, advise, and enable her. These folks slot into a bunch of categories: antagonists, foils, love interests, and so on.

My own failed literary efforts often reveal a basic flaw in my casting process: there are redundancies. I've got two characters performing the same narrative task. The goal should be just the opposite, to cast supporting characters whose roles, in relation to the protagonist, diversify and deepen.

In Kazuo Ishiguro's *Remains of the Day*, for instance, our hero, the British butler Stevens, fixates on Miss Kenton, a fellow servant who once shared his fanatical devotion to the household he serves. Their attraction blossoms into an unrequited romance. Miss Kenton eventually confronts Stevens and intimates her desire for him but is unable to breach his inhibitions. He is too terrified of losing control, which he mistakes for dignity. Still later, Miss Kenton excoriates Stevens for his loyalty to their bigoted employer. She eventually abandons him for a marriage of convenience.

Miss Kenton serves variously as ally, confidant, beloved, foil, and antagonist. By the end of the novel, we see what Stevens can't quite admit to himself: that his motoring tour of Somerset ends in her town precisely because he wishes to win Miss Kenton back. She is the central regret in his life, the chance for happiness sacrificed on the altar of his pride.

IN MY OWN LITERARY TRAVELS, depth of characterization marks the essential difference between published and unpublished work. It is recognizable immediately.

Consider our first encounter with Gatsby, that smile he flashes Nick Carraway, which, we are told, "seemed to face the whole eternal world for an instant, and then concentrated on you with an irresistible prejudice in your favor. It understood you just as far as you wanted to be understood, believed in you as you would like to believe in yourself, and assured you that it had precisely the impression of you that, at your best, you hoped to convey. Precisely at that point it vanished—and I was looking at an elegant young roughneck, a year or two over thirty, whose elaborate formality of speech just missed being absurd."

Nick's sustained focus on a single smile allows us to glimpse the fraudulence and insecurity lurking beneath Gatsby's magnetic charm. Fitzgerald knows his hero better than Gatsby knows himself and is able to convey his core identity with shocking efficiency.

The easiest way to conceptualize *core identity* is to consider someone you know intimately, a parent or a lover or a best friend. Now close your eyes and think about what makes them *them*. Certain details inevitably assert themselves: physical attributes, gestures, colloquialisms, nervous habits.

But it's more than that, isn't it? We have an innate sense of what makes them tick, not just how they present to others but how they think and feel and behave privately.

This wisdom didn't come cheap. It's based on years of observation and an immense trove of data. We know what family they were born into and what role; whether they were the eldest of nine raised by an impoverished single mother or an only child reared by servants in arid prosperity. We know about the expectations placed upon them and the traumas they suffered. We know about their anxieties, obsessions, and phobias, their job history, body issues, spiritual beliefs. We know the uniform they don for work and the costume they slip into for play. We know about the pills lurking in their medicine cabinets and the love letters stashed at the bottom of their steamer trunks.

In my own fiction, I have rarely entered a story with this kind of intel. On the contrary, my early drafts are often filled with getting-to-know-you scenes, in which my protagonist awakens to the shrill of an alarm clock and stumbles through her morning routine, while I frisk the premises for clues as to who the hell she might be. I'm not really writing a story at this point; I'm doing exploratory character work.

I think most of us embark on our stories with an intuitive sense that we will discover our characters by putting them through their paces.

What's more, most of us do this work in a mode known as "indirect characterization," meaning the reader learns about the character through her actions and thoughts at a particular moment in her life.

Direct characterization comes directly from the narrator, who can bluntly report essential facts that would take much longer to convey in scene. Consider Emma Woodhouse, "handsome, clever, and rich, with a comfortable home and happy disposition." We learn that Emma is twenty-one, the youngest of two daughters born to an indulgent father. Her mother is dead, and the governess who raised her is recently married. "The real evils, indeed, of Emma's situation were the power of having rather too much her own way, and a disposition to think a little too well of herself," Austen informs us. "These were the disadvantages which threatened alloy to her many enjoyments. The danger, however, was at present so unperceived, that they did not by any means rank as misfortunes with her."

Translation: Emma is cruising for a bruising.

If I appear to be making a case for the virtues of direct characterization, I am. For years, I confused interiority with intimacy. I assumed that plunking the reader behind a character's eyeballs would grant them access to that character's soul. Austen's narrators prove to be extraordinarily intimate guides precisely because of this capacity for efficient delivery of context, combined with piercing psychological insight.

Direct characterization offers a direct access to the internal conflicts, blind spots, and unconscious motives of your people. This has the magical effect of compelling us to feel protective of them, especially if we have the same internal conflicts, blind spots, and unconscious motives. We identify with Emma because we, too, have struggled with the perils of entitlement.

In works of memoir or personal essay, the goal is for the narrator to conceive of her younger self as a separate entity, a *character* whose experiences the older, presumably wiser, narrator interprets.

In "Goodbye to All That," Joan Didion describes her arrival in New York City at twenty, the way she sits in her freezing hotel room for three days, wrapped in a blanket, trying to get over a cold and a high fever. "It did not occur to me to call a doctor, because I knew none," she observes, "and although it did occur to me to call the desk and ask that the air conditioner be turned off, I never called, because I did not know how much to tip whoever might come—was anyone ever so young? I am here to tell you that someone was." That's the kind of unflinching self-appraisal you need to render yourself as a character.

Of course, there's a whole subset of stories that are energized by unreliable narrators. In such cases, the author's role is to let the protagonist run his or her or their mouth. Humans are programmed to reveal themselves, if not by earnest confession than by ardent denial. Consider the narrator of Matthew Klam's short story "Sam the Cat," an anxious Lothario who can't stop crowing about his conquests: "I've rubbed my hand across bare stomachs from here to Estonia and back. They give the word and it's a free-for-all. If I were a girl, I'd fuck ten guys a day."

When a character is so insistent about his identity, the writer knows precisely how to endanger him. We could give a dude like this any number of afflictions: an unplanned pregnancy, a woman who spurns him, erectile dysfunction. Klam subjects Sam to the ultimate disgrace: a homoerotic attraction he cannot shake, which unmasks the terror lurking beneath his braggadocio. *If I were a girl, I'd fuck ten guys a day.*

I'll reiterate here that we don't have to go deep with every single character in our stories. One of the patterns that I still detect in my early drafts (and encounter routinely in student work) is a tendency to be too democratic with my characterization. Often, I'll spend more words describing a minor character than a major one.

I do this because I don't know yet who my major characters are, or how they fit into the chain of consequence. Providing excess detail creates the illusion that I am crafting a world so vivid even the bit players are 3D. It's a form of stalling that misleads the reader, who is still trying to determine which characters matter enough to be worthy of sympathy.

Major characters deserve an entrance, not just for the reader's benefit, but so that you (the author) can establish their stake in the story, how their motives will interact with those of the other characters.

In my autopsy of the novel *Stoner*, I couldn't help but marvel at the entrance afforded to Hollis Lomax, a celebrated academic whom we first encounter arriving, conspicuously late, to his debut faculty meeting. We see a man "barely over five feet in height" whose body is "grossly misshapen so that he appeared to be always struggling for balance." He stands for several moments "with his blond head downward, as if he were inspecting his highly polished black shoes and the sharp crease of his black trousers." He takes a drag on his cigarette, then looks up so that his rapt audience can at last inspect his face.

"It was the face of a matinee idol," we are told. "Long and thin and mobile, it was nevertheless strongly featured; his forehead was high and narrow, with heavy veins, and his thick waving hair, the color of ripe wheat, swept back from it in a somewhat theatrical pompadour." Everything about Lomax screams *drama*.

Note how quickly he becomes round. His facial beauty and gestural elegance play against his physical disfigurement; his hunger for attention signals an acute awareness of being judged. The message is unmistakable: here is someone powerful yet unstable.

At first, Lomax and Stoner appear destined to become friends. They get drunk and bond over their lonely childhoods and the refuge they found in literature. Later, mortified by the intimacies he's shared, resentful of Stoner's normalcy, Lomax turns against his colleague and spends the rest of the novel bullying him. The seeds of this conduct—the insecure malevolence, the energetic manipulation—are there from the beginning.

THAT'S HOW IT WORKS with strong characterization: the character's actions register as the inevitable outgrowth of their core identity. It's important to emphasize the word *actions* here, because (as Aristotle reminds us) it is action that determines fate.

That may sound like a rather obvious point, but I spent years hacking away at stories in which my protagonists remained stubbornly passive. As a young writer, this often took the form of writing about The Alienated, an exalted breed of character so deeply and mysteriously wounded that they were no longer able to feel much of anything.

The problem with such characters is that alienation is not a natural human resting state; it's a response to thwarted desire. Our duty as writers is not to erect lovely monuments to the lesser defense mechanisms but to dismantle them. Our characters must yearn and act upon their yearnings. Sometimes, these actions are epic in scale. Think Ahab seeking vengeance on Moby Dick. Sometimes the action in question appears utterly mundane. Megha Majumdar's 2020 novel, *A Burning*, stems from a single errant social media post.

Her young heroine, Jivan, is a striver living in the slums of east India. One night, she witnesses a group of terrorists torch a stalled subway train. At home, she goes on Facebook and finds a video of a woman who watched her husband and child perish in the blaze, while policemen idled nearby. Jivan condemns the cops online, but nobody responds. Wounded by this indifference, Jivan posts a more provocative comment.

> If the police didn't help ordinary people like you and me, if the police watched them die, doesn't that mean, *I wrote on Facebook*, that the government is also a terrorist?

A few nights later, the police drag Jivan into custody. Because she's Muslim, like the terrorists, and was at the crime scene, her Facebook post is used to justify her arrest.

A Burning is the story of an injustice. But Majumdar is careful not to flatten Jivan into a blameless martyr. She is a complex young woman: furious at the degradations her family has suffered, needy for attention, short-sighted. To a small but crucial degree, she is complicit in the tragedy that befalls her.

IT'S INTIMIDATING TO ASK that we know our characters as well as we know our beloveds, but it's the right aspiration. If a character is proving prickly on a first date, we should be open to considering anything that might help us understand why: romantic history, intimacy issues, the model of love learned from parents.

Often, when I prescribe such considerations, students will say things like, *I don't want to have to psychoanalyze all my characters.* I don't want you to psychoanalyze your characters, either. The pleasure of storytelling is that the author boils away all the fruit-less session work and delivers only the vital moments of trans-formation and self-revelation.

We should approach our characters with a passionate curios-ity, asking not just *What would they do in this situation?* But *Why are they behaving in this way?*

In the drafting of my most recent novel, I invoked this pro-cess every time a new character emerged. At a certain point, to my shock and dismay, I realized that Nancy Reagan was going to be central to the action. I had spent forty years flattening the former First Lady into a caricature, a modern Marie Antoinette hooked on couture and astrology.

As a novelist, I had to start asking who Nancy might be, beyond my bigoted version. This required more than curiosity. I had to study her history to understand how she might see the world.

In the end, my Nancy Reagan—the character, not the person—was a kind of prophet. She believed her husband was destined to lead the country, but she was acutely aware of the danger this put him in, even if he wasn't. Two months into his presidency, Reagan was shot by a would-be assassin. Nancy arrived at the hospital to discover a bullet lodged a quarter of an inch from her husband's heart. And so she did what any of us would do in such a situation: she adopted a belief system that she felt would keep her partner safe. This was how I came to under-stand, and even admire, Nancy Reagan's faith in astrology.

My intention wasn't to excuse any of the despicable things Nancy Reagan did in my novel, or in real life. I was simply trying to acknowledge the sacred parts of her identity, which I couldn't condemn because they were a part of my identity, too.

I, too, had spent years obsessing over our national destiny, pining for a president worthy of our promise. I, too, knew what it was like to love a partner who was vulnerable in ways only I could see.

WE'VE SPENT A BIT MORE TIME than I would have wished talking about Nancy Reagan, but I want to make one more Nancy-adjacent point. Part of the reason I found Nancy fascinating—though I didn't realize this at the time—was because she suffered a terrible internal conflict: She wanted her husband to be president. But that ambition put a target on his back.

This may be the most lucrative question we can ask when it comes to our characters: Where are they in conflict with themselves? More precisely: What are the dangers bound to their desires? Once you've figured that out, you have the link that connects character to plot.

The feeling I'm always after when I read a story is that the people I'm reading about (I don't really think of them as characters) are behaving precisely as their motives dictate. Even the ones who act cruel and destructive have constructed a worldview in which their actions are justified, even heroic. The author's job isn't to absolve any of her major characters, but to reveal them in sufficient depth that we recognize ourselves. *How sad*, I think. *How true. I would have done the same thing.*

A WRINKLE IN TIME

HOW TO MANAGE CHRONOLOGY

From a temporal standpoint, our lives proceed in one direction. From a psychic and emotional standpoint, we're all over the place. Rarely do we live in the present. We live in our memories and our fantasies, our fears and regrets, what happened five minutes ago and what might happen next year. This makes storytelling tricky. If you proceed strictly by time stamp, you're missing out on this simultaneity. If you hopscotch around without clear guidance, your reader will get disoriented.

Alas, chronology ranks pretty low on the standard list of authorial anxieties, compared to plot, character, and so on. I gave it very little thought when I was working on short stories and essays. But as I embarked on longer narratives, I came to see that my job wasn't to manage just characters and events, but time itself. It was Gabriel García Márquez who opened my eyes on this. I kept thinking about his famous opening to *One Hundred Years of Solitude*:

Many years later, as he faced the firing squad, Colonel Aureliano Buendía was to remember that distant afternoon when his father took him to discover ice.

That a novel could begin this way struck me as audacious. The initial clause ("Many years later") throws the action into the future, so that the reader enters the story seconds before a central character's death, then immediately reels back decades to capture an indelible childhood memory. In effect, this sentence operates as a time loop, signaling to the reader that this novel will be told on an epic scale, spiraling through time as required to capture how the past intrudes upon the present.

I HAD A SIMILAR REACTION to Natasha Trethewey's 2020 memoir, *Memorial Drive*. "The last image of my mother, but for the photographs taken of her body at the crime scene, is the formal portrait made only a few months before her death," Trethewey begins. "Perhaps she intended to look back on it years later and say, 'That's where it began, my new life.'"

Like Márquez, Trethewey weds two time frames: her mother sitting for a portrait, and the murder she will suffer months later. The passage confirms a pending calamity while also promising an investigation of the past: the how and why of this awful outcome. Trethewey then introduces a third time frame, an imagined future from which her mother (still alive) gazes upon this portrait as a marker of her new life. The wrenching irony of the passage is a direct result of how Trethewey manages chronology.

Thanks to a series of daring decisions, the reader understands that the story they're reading is really a series of stories, set in different eras, all of which the narrator will be coordinating on their behalf. In fact, these openings clarify the true meaning of "chronology" in storytelling, which isn't the chronological sequence of events in a story, but *how the author decides to present these events* to the reader.

Consider a common fairy tale. In the traditional telling of Cinderella, the events are set out in the order they occurred: Cinderella's mom dies, dad remarries, wicked stepmother moves in, and so on. But there are moments further on in the story—the appearance of Cinderella's fairy godmother, for instance, or the panicky toll of midnight at the ball—that an author might decide make for a more dramatic opening. This decision is entirely up to you. It's your story. What matters is that you are conscious of this decision and its consequences.

Here are the two essential questions to consider:

- Where, in the larger flow of events, have I chosen to enter the story?

- How did my central character arrive at this moment, and what's at stake for her?

If you're going to begin with the clock chiming twelve, and Cinderella hobbling for the palace exit in one glass slipper, the reader is going to need a lot of context.

THIS IS QUITE EASY TO DISCERN when the author knows all the events of the story. (That's why we chose a fairy tale.) The problem with our own stories is that their full scope often emerges only in the writing. In our initial drafts, we're still figuring out what happens, and to whom, the basic sequence of events.

As the larger arc of the story reveals itself, it's worth considering a more fundamental question: What are *all* the events that bear on the fate of the characters in my story? To demonstrate what I mean, consider Meg Wolitzer's novel *The Wife*, which opens with this humdinger:

> The moment I decided to leave him, the moment I thought, enough, we were thirty-five thousand feet above the ocean, hurtling forward but giving the illusion of stillness and tranquility. *Just like our marriage*, I could have said, but why ruin everything right now?

Wolitzer creates suspense by entering the story at the pivotal moment when our narrator, Joan Castleman, decides to end her long marriage. In a sardonic tone, Joan establishes two periods that will eventually converge: the past, in which she falls in love with her (already married) professor, Joe Castleman, helps him become a famous novelist, and gradually sours on their union; and the present, in which Joan must summon the nerve to leave him. Based on this opening, the reader intuitively recognizes how the narrator will manage time, by pivoting back and forth.

Joan doesn't restrict herself to her own experiences. She delves further into the past, relating the story of Joe Castleman's childhood, the sudden death of his father, and how this left him to be doted upon by his mother and aunts, initiating a lifelong dependence on female adoration. This does not excuse Joe Castleman's compulsive infidelity. But it does allow us to understand why he can't grow up or take responsibility for his adultery. Joan also plumbs her own history. We discover that she was drawn to Joe because he activated her literary gifts and offered an escape from the suffocating conformity her wealthy parents enforced.

It's important to acknowledge that young Joan Castleman did not understand her marriage in this way. Only in looking back over many decades can she discern how she and Joe leapt into marriage, driven by anxieties and childish fantasies. This is why Wolitzer opens the novel toward the very end of the story's chronological arc—because it has taken Joan this long to understand *why* she must leave her husband.

IF THE AUTHOR IS DOING HER JOB in managing chronology, the reader isn't thinking about any of this. They are immersed in whatever part of the story the narrator has set before them. They are happily time traveling. When the reader becomes conscious of time, or, more precisely, *confused* about time, it signals the mismanagement of chronology.

The most common symptom I encounter as a teacher is a wrinkled chronology. We start in summer of 2014, then scroll back three years to backfill context, then leap ahead to an undefined era in the future. Amid this frantic movement, the reader becomes unmoored.

There are simple ways to fix these problems. Providing background upfront so you don't have to continually plunge into the past, for instance. Making sure the narrator grounds each scene in a specific era.

A lot of managing chronology boils down to recognizing the move from exposition to scene as a shift in chronological orientation. We are asking the reader to transition from "general time," in which the narrator summarizes many events, over an extended period, to "specific time," in which we enter character experience at a particular moment. It's the difference between reading the words "Long ago, in a galaxy far, far away . . ." at the beginning of *Star Wars* versus watching Darth Vader capture Princess Leia.

This is why I advise writers to compile a timeline of all the events that bear on your story—because this process allows you to draw back and consider which events deserve to be rendered in scene and which are best summarized.

Flashbacks and flash-forwards are tricky because they represent mini wrinkles in time. They are most effective when the reader feels securely grounded in time and when the memory, or fantasy, arises from some distinct trigger in the present. That is, when the shift feels organically experienced by the character rather than engineered by the author.

As our heroine stands before the ocean at dusk, watching her only child get married (for instance), we have to trust that our readers will track her memories and associations, so long as they understand what has instigated them. Does the occasion call to mind her first wedding? Does the smell of scallops wrapped in bacon evoke the glorious pregnancy cravings she suffered carrying her daughter? Does the molten light on the ocean make her think about the fires that will consume her body, if she signs the cremation papers her oncologist gently suggested she have drawn up, which she has slipped into her purse, right beside the speech she intends to deliver at the reception?

TIME MANAGEMENT IS AN AUTHORIAL DUTY that gets delegated to the narrator. In *The Wife*, that means Joan Castleman is in charge. But in a novel such as *Americanah*, Chimamanda Ngozi Adichie faces a steeper challenge. The story shifts between two close third points of view, those of high school lovers Ifemelu and Obinze, tracking them across three decades and as many continents. It's a lot to manage.

Adichie does so by creating an anchoring scene: the novel begins with Ifemelu heading to a salon to have her hair braided. After thirteen years in America, she's on the brink of returning to Nigeria, and encountering Obinze, who has repatriated from England. Adichie spends more than half the book detailing how the two lovers came together, how they fell apart, and the tumultuous lives they led as immigrants. All the while, the reader remains grounded in the "present" of the hair salon, where the novel's themes (race, immigration, the precarious pursuit of partnership for Nigerian women) play out in specific time.

Readers are always happiest when they feel grounded, both in a particular moment *and* in the larger arc of a story. Cheryl

Strayed opens her memoir, *Wild*, with a catastrophe: thirty-eight days into a solo hike along the Pacific Crest Trail, her boot bounces over a cliff and disappears into the forest below. In a fit of exasperation, she heaves her second boot. Then we get this:

> I was alone. I was barefoot. I was twenty-six years old and an orphan too. . . . My father left my life when I was six. My mother died when I was twenty-two. In the wake of her death, my stepfather morphed from the person I considered my dad into a man I only occasionally recognized. My two siblings scattered in their grief, in spite of my efforts to hold us together, until I gave up and scattered as well.
>
> In the years before I pitched my boot over the edge of that mountain, I'd been pitching myself over the edge too. I'd ranged and roamed and railed—from Minnesota to New York to Oregon and all across the West—until at last I found myself, bootless, in the summer of 1995, not so much loose in the world as bound to it.

In two paragraphs, Strayed has forged the chronological outline of her story and specified the events that drove her to hike the PCT, an experience that would "both make me into the woman I knew I could become and turn me back into the girl I'd once been." It's important to acknowledge that Strayed wrote *Wild* over many years and published it a decade and a half after her walkabout. She had a lot of time to think about how to manage time in her story.

My own drafts invariably lack this perspective. I'm thinking here of a passage that my wife, Erin, flagged, after reading an early version of my novel *All the Secrets of the World*. It was about how much my teenage heroine yearned for the trust of the older man bent on seducing her. The problem was that this insight arrived 457 pages into the book. In other words, I had obscured the central desire driving this relationship because it hadn't *occurred to me* until page 457. I immediately rewrote the first hundred pages of the novel.

The same pattern prevails in the manuscripts I edit. This is especially true in nonfiction projects, where writers often unconsciously suppress events and dynamics too painful to recount. Several years ago, for instance, I edited a memoir about a pioneering female doctor. The material was captivating. But the chronology was so chaotic that I kept falling out of the story. I found myself asking: *Why am I hearing this part of the story now?* And, just as often, *Why didn't I hear this part of the story earlier?*

The author described a career marked by vicious feuds with male colleagues. But we learned only at the very end of the book that she had been abandoned by her beloved father, at age seven. And that she had felt enraged, even then, by the monstrous double standards that demanded her obedience while granting the boys around her freedom. Knowing these facts would have helped me understand her explosive reactions to the casual sexism of male doctors.

I don't mean to suggest that the writer had to tell her story in chronological order. I would have been quite pleased if she moved from a moment of conflict in her workplace to a memory of her childhood, when she first encountered patriarchal suppression. That's what the astute management of chronology is really about: finding those moments when the past and present reveal themselves as connected.

THERE IS ALWAYS "considerable tension between chronology and theme," John McPhee observes. But sometimes an author wants to write in a way that privileges theme over chronology. Jennifer Egan's *A Visit from the Goon Squad* zooms between eras and characters. The connective tissue of the novel is thematic: the ways in which time assaults our dreams. Because of how Egan orders her chapters, readers are continually encountering characters whose youthful hopes have been obliterated by aging, loss, and regret. Like the characters, we experience the ravages of time as abrupt and violent.

Still other books pointedly seek to disrupt our perception of time as strictly linear. Kurt Vonnegut's *Slaughterhouse-Five* begins with these lines:

> Listen: Billy Pilgrim has become unstuck in time. Billy has gone to sleep a senile widower and awakened on his wedding day. He has walked through a door in 1955 and come out another one in 1941. He has gone back through that door to find himself in 1963. He has seen his birth and death many times, he says, and pays random visits to all the events in between.

Billy's relatives regard his unique relationship to time as a symptom of post-traumatic stress disorder, resulting from his experiences as a prisoner of war during the bombing of Dresden. But Billy insists that he was abducted by aliens, who live in a dimension in which past, present, and future coexist. Regardless of what the reader decides to believe, the novel remains faithful to Billy's conception of time. It is told in fragments, as our hero ping-pongs through his history.

This is what makes *Slaughterhouse-Five* so groundbreaking. The book's chronology is relentlessly and intentionally mangled. Yet Vonnegut's omniscient narrator manages time masterfully. We know where we are, in time and space, at every moment. The fragments are carefully arranged so that—amid the philosophical musings and extraterrestrial digressions—the novel drives steadily toward the historical trauma haunting Billy: the bombing of Dresden.

The lesson is this: our stories needn't be captives to an orderly chronology. There is a little Billy Pilgrim in all of us. As storytellers, it is our job to make discernible how and why our characters become "unstuck in time." Ultimately, we want our readers to trust that we have selected the moments from each life most worthy of examination, the ones our characters will never forget and are thus destined to revisit.

GETTING THE READER IN THE CAR

A SURVEY OF BRILLIANT OPENING PARAGRAPHS AND SCATTERED THOUGHTS THEREON

Let me start by stating something I hope we all have in common, which is that I find writing excruciating, a form of self-imposed exile with a side order of shingles. I would rather do almost anything other than write. If you are one of those people who doesn't agree with this statement, who finds the hours spent at the keyboard sailing past, well then, I am happy for you in the exact same way you are happy for the person who married your soulmate.

Not having, as yet, established a subject, I will now proceed to a digression entitled Things I Do to Avoid Writing, an area of inquiry expansive enough to accommodate its own essay, or perhaps memoir:

1. Google myself

2. Lament photos of myself that appear on Google

3. Review my list of enemies

4. Curse the many editors who refuse to respond to my emails

5. Compose elaborately casual and nonetheless imploring emails attempting to elicit a response to my previous email

6. Urinate

6a. Ponder if I urinate too much

7. Recall, with the peculiar fondness of middle age, my last colonoscopy, and mull whether it was appropriate for me to say to the doctor, just before he put me under, "Aren't you going to buy me dinner first?"

8. Contemplate my integrity

9. Wander upstairs for a snack

10. Brood over why my children have no respect for me

11. Consider an elaborately casual and nonetheless imploring email to my children

12. Engage my wife in some complaint related to topics 1–11, until such a time as she asks me to repair something

The list goes on, so let me skip ahead to my all-time favorite form of procrastination, which is wandering to my bookcase and reading the first page of a cherished book.

What I'm looking for is the jolt of that opening graph, the sense of assurance, of destiny, the staggering promise. It's an unconscious ritual intended to remind me what literature can do, which is to offer a deeper way of thinking and feeling in the world. But how in God's name can I experience that in a single paragraph? How can prose feel so intuitively right as to create the piercing momentary delusion that writing is effortless? That's the miracle we'll be taking up.

Let's begin with a big stupid generalization. For the most part, writers and readers are looking for different things in an opening paragraph.

Writers want the following: to establish intimacy with the characters we're writing about (especially the protagonist), which we assume will imply authority. We want to convince the reader, rather too ardently, that we are crafting a tale worth reading. We are naturally inclined toward the belief that opening in scene is more compelling than exposition and that a rush of vivid sensory detail is preferable to the measured dispensation of information. We would rather dazzle than inform.

Readers are less concerned with intimacy. They're not even especially eager for dazzle. What they want is communion with a wise and dangerous mind, the promise of a good story, and the assurance that they are going to be taken care of, rather than taken for granted.

There is no set formula as to how these aims can be accomplished. But as I reexamined my favorite opening graphs, clear patterns emerged. First, great openings never, or almost never, confuse the reader. On the contrary, they seek to establish a relationship of *informational equity* between the reader and the characters. If anything, they offer the reader more information than the characters possess.

From the Per Olov Enquist novel *The Visit of the Royal Physician*:

> On April 5, 1768, Johann Friedrich Struensee was appointed Royal Physician to King Christian VII of Denmark, and four years later he was executed.

That's the entire first paragraph, an unvarnished statement of fact regarding an obscure historical episode. Why do I find it so thrilling? First, because it contains a potent and nearly invisible irony: the man called upon to heal an ailing monarch winds up murdered by his patient. Second, because the reader inevitably ponders how and why this gruesome event transpires and is therefore left in a keen state of curiosity.

Another way of saying this is that we can embed with a character only if we understand the dangers they face, right from the jump. Consider how Alicia Erian opens *Towelhead*:

> My mother's boyfriend got a crush on me, so she sent me to live with Daddy. I didn't want to live with Daddy. He had a weird accent and came from Lebanon. My mother

met him in college, then they got married and had me, then they got divorced when I was five. My mother told me it was because my father was cheap and bossy. When my parents got divorced, I wasn't upset. I had a memory of Daddy slapping my mother, and then of my mother taking off his glasses and grinding them into the floor with her shoe. I don't know what they were fighting about, but I was glad that he couldn't see anymore.

Note how much vital context our teenage heroine, Jasira, imparts:

- She's a child of divorce who has begun to attract the men around her.

- Her mother gets involved with destructive men, fails to protect Jasira from a predatory boyfriend, and in fact exiles her.

- Jasira, who is half Lebanese, doesn't want to live with her immigrant father.

- Her parents split amid emotional and physical violence, which Jasira witnessed and internalized at a very young age.

None of this registers as an *info dump*—the dreaded term invoked to describe background that feels inessential, redundant, or premature. On the contrary, Erian has launched us into the story with incredible velocity, simply by allowing her heroine to summarize her situation. A vulnerable, angry teen wise to the power of her sexuality. What could go wrong?

My hunch as a reader is confirmed by my experience as a writer. Authorial assurance can't be faked. If I don't know the story I want to tell, at least in its rough outlines, anxiety gets the best of me. I start to embellish the language, to leap from scene to scene in search of epiphanies and eloquence. I start trying to stuff the reader into the trunk of a car.

The best openings induce the exact opposite feeling: as if the author is merely standing by the door of a gleaming vehicle, with a ribbon of road leading toward some dark territory of revelation, shaking her head at the notion that I would miss out on the trip.

So one question for all of us to consider is: Does your first paragraph offer readers a clear sense of the story they're going to hear? Does it set out the context and stakes? That's the essential vibe I crave: that the author is not afraid to go big at the beginning.

This impulse prevails especially when a writer is introducing a world that operates differently from our own. From Ursula K. Le Guin's classic fantasy *A Wizard of Earthsea*:

> The island of Gont, a single mountain that lifts its peak a mile above the storm-racked Northeast Sea, is a land famous for wizards.

"First sentences are doors to worlds," is how Le Guin puts it. Writers of speculative fiction are smart to begin the work of world-building immediately, in particular when the world in question contradicts our own history, as in Philip Roth's *The Plot Against America*:

> Fear presides over these memories, a perpetual fear. Of course no childhood is without its terrors, yet I wonder if I would have been a less frightened boy if Lindbergh hadn't been president or if I hadn't been the offspring of Jews.

We know the voice guiding us is looking back into a distant and terrible past and has had time to reflect. But we're most struck by how differently this world operates. Likewise, in Orwell's *1984* ("It was a bright cold day in April, and the clocks were striking thirteen") and Bradbury's *Fahrenheit 451* ("It was a pleasure to burn").

These graphs scan superficially as "shockers." But the authors' intentions are just the opposite: to orient. They understand that it would be confusing and counterproductive to immerse the reader in any one consciousness until we understand the lay of the land.

But what if we're talking about a story driven by personal, rather than historical, upheaval? Let's let Sylvia Plath field that one. She begins *The Bell Jar* with a searing, firsthand account of the disturbances prowling inside Esther Greenwood.

> It was a queer, sultry summer, the summer they electrocuted the Rosenbergs, and I didn't know what I was doing in New York. I'm stupid about executions. The idea of being electrocuted makes me sick, and that's all there was

to read about in the papers—goggle-eyed headlines staring up at me on every street corner and at the fusty, peanut-smelling mouth of every subway. It had nothing to do with me, but I couldn't help wondering what it would be like, being burned alive all along your nerves.

Plath goes big here in several ways. She sets out the basic context (addled young woman, summer, New York), in a distinct voice (wry, post-adolescent, self-doubting) that delivers vivid and unsettling details. The exact destination isn't stated, but the direction is clearly ominous. By the fourth sentence, we've burrowed deeply enough into Esther's consciousness to access the darkest invasive thought in her life and to understand her disavowal ("it had nothing to do with me") as evidence of her incipient madness.

At the other end of the spectrum is a novel such as *Mrs. Bridge* by Evan S. Connell:

Her first name was India—she was never able to get used to it. It seemed to her that her parents must have been thinking of someone else when they named her. Or were they hoping for another sort of daughter? As a child she was often on the point of inquiring, but time passed and she never did.

This doesn't register as a "voice-driven" paragraph, as we've come to define that term. It can hardly be said to promise action, at least in the form of external conflict. But there's tremendous tension here, because Connell's detached appraisal yields a painfully intimate portrait of his heroine. It takes him four sentences to establish her insecurity, her personal dislocation, and her ambivalent wish to confront her doubts. Knowing Mrs. Bridge as he does, Connell presents scenes that continually hound her ambivalence. This opening not only foreshadows and encapsulates, it *instigates* the rest of the book.

Austen does the same thing in *Emma*. Once we know that Emma Woodhouse is a spoiled and meddling young woman, we know where the story is headed.

For a sparkling nonfiction example, let's turn to Henry David Thoreau's *Walden*:

When I wrote the following pages, or rather the bulk of them, I lived alone, in the woods, a mile from any neighbor, in a house which I had built myself, on the shore of Walden Pond, in Concord, Massachusetts, and earned my living by the labor of my hands only. I lived there two years and two months. At present I am a sojourner in civilized life again.

Thoreau could have opened with a rant about self-sufficiency, an aphorism about nonconformity, some account of his hijinks with a critter or an arrogant city slicker, even a walk through the woods at dusk. Instead, he sets out the precise parameters of his experiment—its terms, location, and duration—and trusts the reader to come along. The only hint of attitude is the subversive wink of that final line.

I'm not suggesting that subjective, immersive openings are doomed. But it's worth noting their limitations. Here's how Don DeLillo began his debut novel, *Americana*:

Then we came to the end of another dull and lurid year. Lights were strung across the front of every shop. Men selling chestnuts wheeled their smoky carts. In the evenings the crowds were immense and traffic built to a tidal roar. The santas of Fifth Avenue rang their little bells with an odd sad delicacy, as if sprinkling salt on some brutally spoiled piece of meat. Music came from all the stores in jingles, chants and hosannas, and from the Salvation Army bands came the martial trumpet lament of ancient Christian legions. It was a strange sound to hear in that time and place, the smack of cymbals and high-collared drums, a suggestion that children were being scolded for a bottomless sin, and it seemed to annoy people. But the girls were lovely and undismayed, shopping in every mad store, striding through those magnetic twilights like drum majorettes, tall and pink, bright packages cradled to their tender breasts. The blind man's German shepherd slept through it all.

I love this opening for its remarkably vivid powers of observation. But do I have any idea what this book is going to be about? Not really. As it turns out, the plot of *Americana* is strikingly similar to *On the Road* by Jack Kerouac: restless young men set out on a cross-country trip in a search of what DeLillo calls "the big outdoor soul of America." Check out how carefully the freewheeling Kerouac preps us for the journey:

> I first met Dean not long after my wife and I split up. I had just gotten over a serious illness that I won't bother to talk about, except that it had something to do with the miserably weary split-up and my feeling that everything was dead. With the coming of Dean Moriarty began the part of my life you could call my life on the road. Before that I'd often dreamed of going West to see the country, always vaguely planning and never taking off.

This is Kerouac at his best: urgent, candid, tremendously attendant to the needs of the reader. It's this generosity that makes *On the Road* a classic. For all his virtuosity, DeLillo stuffs us in the trunk.

I pulled the same maneuver in each of my own bungled novels, though the trunks I crafted were more claustrophobic than radiant. It was only as a short story writer that I began to trust in the power of going big at the outset. And even then, I hardly realized it was happening, because I was mostly just imitating the stories I adored, their audacious patience and confidence. Michael Cunningham's *White Angel* leaps to mind:

> We lived then in Cleveland, in the middle of everything. It was the sixties—our radios sang out love all day long. This of course is history. It happened before the city of Cleveland went broke, before its river caught fire. We were four. My

mother and father, Carlton, and me. Carlton turned sixteen the year I turned nine. Between us were several brothers and sisters, weak flames quenched in our mother's
womb. We are not a fruitful or many-branched line. Our
family name is Morrow.

When I first encountered this paragraph, I couldn't stop reading it. The stark, declarative sentences, the mood of impending
doom. The events didn't feel recounted so much as ordained. I
could hear the same music, in a more jittery register, when I read
Rock Springs by Richard Ford:

Edna and I had started down from Kalispell, heading for
Tampa-St. Pete where I still had some friends from the old
glory days who wouldn't turn me in to the police. I had
managed to scrape with the law in Kalispell over several
bad checks—which is a prison crime in Montana. And I
knew Edna was already looking at her cards and thinking
about a move, since it wasn't the first time I'd been in law
scrapes in my life. She herself had already had her own
troubles, losing her kids and keeping her ex-husband,
Danny, from breaking in her house and stealing her things
while she was at work, which was really why I had moved
in in the first place, that and needing to give my little
daughter, Cheryl, a better shake in things.

Note how the simple recitation of facts here creates tension:
our narrator is a criminal on the lam, his relationship is in trouble, he has a daughter to look after. The sensible part of us would

never get into a car with this guy. We'd be more likely to dial the cops and report him. But the part of us that reads isn't sensible. It craves danger. Great openings recognize this. They make us desperate to ride along.

I'll conclude this harried survey with my favorite opening in all of literature. I love it especially because it is so radically different from the other examples I've cited:

"Where's Papa going with that ax?" said Fern to her mother as they were setting the table for breakfast.

"Out to the hoghouse," replied Mrs. Arable. "Some pigs were born last night."

"I don't see why he needs an ax," continued Fern, who was only eight.

Yes, E. B. White has begun his novel with a burst of dialogue. Yes, we're in the midst of a scene. But what matters here is that ax, and Fern's instinctive suspicion of it. When she learns that her father plans to kill the runt of the litter, she dashes outside and attempts to snatch the blade out of her father's hands. "The pig couldn't help being born small, could it?" she asks him. "If *I* had been very small at birth, would you have killed *me*?"

Staggered by this query, John Arable appears "almost ready to cry himself." He grants a stay of execution, awarding Fern custody of the tiny pig she will christen Wilbur.

With this opening, White has captured both the event that jump-starts the plot of *Charlotte's Web* and the singular moment when a child instigates a moral disruption in the adult world. Along with John Arable, we are forced to confront the illusion of human dominion, to consider the possibility that the animals we yoke and slaughter have their own rich world of dreams and dreads and friendship.

How you begin your next story is entirely up to you. There is no one right way to get the reader into the car. But I urge you to consider the nature of your invitation. Be as swift as possible in apprising us of the pleasures and hazards to come. Be as kind as Charlotte is to Wilbur, as bold and guileless as Fern when she leaps for that ax.

EVERY STORY NEEDS A TELLER

MEET YOUR GREATEST GIFT TO READERS,
THE NARRATOR

Long ago, when I was teaching fiction workshops at Emerson College, I began to encounter a particular species of student story. The hero was an unnamed man, often unshaven, who woke in a strange hotel or bar or dorm room with no idea where he was or why. Invariably, something traumatic had happened to him and to *her*, a mysterious female pronoun—presumably his beloved. Our hero didn't know exactly what had happened though, because, as would eventually emerge, he suffered from anterograde amnesia, a rare form of short-term memory loss that afflicts vast numbers of fictional characters. In an effort to remain loyal to the protagonist's disorientation, the remainder of the story consisted of fragmented scenes, chronologically mutilated for maximum profundity.

My standard reaction to these pieces was to jot earnestly flummoxed queries in the margins such as "Where are we?" and "Are the italics supposed to be flashbacks?" and "Is it possible I'm missing a page?" Then office hours would roll around and the author in question would appear and I would say, "I found your story really ambitious, but I'm not sure I totally understood it."

The author would look at me, with pity, and utter the six words I eventually learned to dread: "Have you seen the movie *Memento*?"

No, I would say, I hadn't seen that one. They would explain that their story was inspired by *Memento*. Then they would recite the plot of the film while I sat quietly in my adjunct cubicle mulling suicide.

This was all happening back in the dark ages of the internet. No social media or Wi-Fi. Cell phones were still dumb. My students read books, when assigned to do so by well-meaning primitives such as myself. But movies and TV shows were the art that inhabited them.

In the years since, I've worked with students who are dedicated readers. And yet I continue to encounter manuscripts with far too much vivid camera work and far too little actual storytelling. Vital information has been withheld, and the result, I often feel, is that I am not being told a story at all, so much as being asked to solve a puzzle.

For a while, I was sure this had to do with how creative writing is taught, and specifically the sustained dogma against exposition that finds its purest expression in that well-meaning mantra *show, don't tell*. But I've come to believe that the dwindling of strong, independent narrators in modern fiction is also the result of larger shifts in the culture. Specifically, its abject domination by frantic visual media.

FOR MOST OF HUMAN HISTORY, we've relied on storytellers. Their myths and histories offered a cohesive vision of our origins, our moral codes, our mortal fate. Eventually these stories were preserved, duplicated, and made portable. The teller was supplanted by the writer, who deployed a guide called the narrator. As writers sought to reckon with the growing complexity of human affairs, they relied more and more on this figure.

The narrators in a novel by Eliot or Dickens or Tolstoy, for instance, display remarkable latitude. They portray how individual fates collide with history, how the orphan survives amid the Industrial Revolution, how lives are brought low by war. These stories offer a sweeping depiction of the world that helps us clarify our role in it.

The advent of modernism drastically reduced the narrator's jurisdiction. Writers like James Joyce and Gertrude Stein turned their gaze inward, toward the intricacies of consciousness. At the other extreme was Hemingway, whose central innovation as a stylist was the crafting of short declarative sentences that conveyed deep emotion and psychology. "Prose is architecture, not interior decoration, and the Baroque is over." That was his decree. You didn't let some loudmouth tell the reader that Nick Adams is a traumatized veteran, or that the young couple swilling Anis del Toros and gazing miserably at those white hills are talking about abortion. To do so was an imaginative surrender.

Hemingway attributed the emotional reticence of his work to the trauma of World War I. It's also true that Hemingway was among the first writers born into the age of motion pictures. In his world, the narrator acts as something like an invisible movie camera.

These days, most writers spend a lot more time talking about movies and TV shows than they do about novels. Not because we've become hopelessly shallow but because visual stories are far easier to consume and talk about. Our reactions to them are less personal and nuanced than our reactions to books. Thus, they're more unifying as cultural narratives.

These programs are the result of hundreds of artists collaborating to create a tantalizing and entirely artificial world: cinematographers, sound technicians, actors, musicians, set designers, and so on. Every single moment has been meticulously engineered for maximum aesthetic impact. The plots and character arcs and set pieces and showdowns—all brilliantly conceived and refined and realized, every riposte, every gesture, every shadow, every beat. Every show, even the *bad* ones, represents a colossal and collective act of attention.

What most of them don't have is a narrator. Why bother? The viewer can almost always figure out the setting and the relationships between the characters because they are able to *see and hear them*. There are always important events happening to push the plot forward—double crosses, dead bodies, extramarital affairs—events that can be dramatized. The characters are always presented within specific social, geographic, and professional milieus.

Writers have only one collaborator: the reader. She knows nothing at the start: who's speaking to her, who the characters are, where they are, how they're related, what's at stake in the story. She arrives eager for immersion but has to imagine an entire world into existence using only the words we supply.

And thus contemporary writers, steeped in the audiovisual dazzlement of TV and movies, are likely to feel an immediate and crushing sense of insecurity. This led my Emerson students to appropriate elements from their favorite films. More often the mimesis is unconscious. The writer instinctually jettisons the narrator, blows past exposition, and begins amid the rising action. Our readers wind up in the same state of unproductive bewilderment as I was, sitting in my sad little adjunct cubicle.

IN THE ABSENCE OF an independent narrator, the only way for the writer to convey information is by having the protagonist *think it*, or by placing it in the mouths of your poor characters in the form of informational quotes. Your characters, at this point, aren't characters at all. They're incredibly self-conscious and inefficient tools of narration.

When we provide action before narration, our scenes suffer, too. Writers leap into the fray, hoping to hook the reader. At some point, they realize the reader doesn't know enough to experience the emotional significance of the scene, causing them to awkwardly backfill the exposition that should have come first. This blunts the forward momentum of the scene.

By narrator, I do not mean author. The author exists outside the text. He or she deploys the narrator, who lives within the text. This distinction holds even in the case of nonfiction.

Regardless of genre or point of view, the narrator's purpose is the same: to act as the ultimate show runner, to set out for the reader the story's logical flow, the relevant histories, natures, and motives of the characters, the prevailing properties and customs of the world in question, and certain insights into human nature traceable to the author. When the story moves into scene, the narrator swoops into a more subjective mode.

My students often struggle to understand what, precisely, the reader needs to know, and when. They worry that I am asking them to spend their precious early paragraphs on dental records. I'm not. (Unless you're writing a book that hinges on dental records!) I just want to know enough to feel what I'm being shown. Because characters do not live in a world composed of vagaries. They take shape, or should take shape, within a precise set of dramatic circumstances—of which your loyal reader should be apprised.

It is not my intention to advocate for a particular mode of narration. But it's worth noting the basic trade-off involved. Close narrators (whether first- or third-person) privilege subjective interiority. Distant, or objective, narration offers greater perspective. From *Anna Karenina*:

All happy families are alike; each unhappy family is unhappy in its own way.

All was confusion in the Oblonskys' house. The wife had found out that the husband was having an affair with their former French governess, and had announced to the husband that she could not live in the same house with him. This situation had continued for three days now, and was painfully felt by the couple themselves, as well as by all the members of the family and household.

Why not just start with the adulterous tumult, which so elegantly prefigures what's to come for Anna? Because Tolstoy wants to establish a narrator capable of issuing sweeping declarations about human nature. At the same time, he understands that readers want to be inside the hearts and minds and bodies of his characters in moments of peak emotion, such as the ballroom scene where Anna experiences her initial, powerful attraction to Vronsky, while Kitty suffers his devastating rejection.

Writers achieve this latitude in a variety of ways. In *The Great Gatsby*, Fitzgerald offers a secondary character as a kind of authorial stand-in. Nick Carroway identifies with his friend Gatsby but recognizes the nature of his folly. Others shift between close first-person narrators (Faulkner's *As I Lay Dying*, for example, or Megha Majumdar's *A Burning*) or third-person perspectives (*Wide Sargasso Sea* by Jean Rhys), creating a choral effect.

The goal isn't to find the right narrator, but the right *narrative stance*, one supple enough to shift perspectives, from the omniscient and measured to the subjective and unhinged.

THIS RELATIONSHIP with a particular voice, the narrator, distinguishes literature from every other art form. It's a relationship readers hunger for immediately, in all genres. The central pleasure of nonfiction doesn't reside in the events recounted but the narrator's ability to reflect on them, to pluck meaning from the rush of experience.

In her memoir *Easy Beauty*, the philosopher Chloé Cooper Jones chronicles her life with the congenital condition sacral agenesis. Born "a ball of twisted muscle and tucked bone," her body is a source of constant pain and the object of routine humiliations. In her pursuit of beauty in its variegated forms, she travels from a Roman statue garden to a Beyoncé concert.

The book soars not because of its jet-setting, or the author's agonizing condition, but because the narrator is such an enthralling companion, determined to understand the cultural mechanics of beauty and, at the same time, ruthlessly self-interrogating. "We seek beauty, but our understanding of its nature is limited," she observes. "We find it primarily in easy-to-appreciate human forms. As we grow older and learn more, we journey closer to the truth of beauty. We begin to perceive it more powerfully in minds than in bodies. We stay on our quest, ascending, going higher and higher in our conception of beauty. As we do, our capacity to recognize beauty grows larger. We can take in more." At last, our eyes adjust and "we become part of a bigger sum, something vast and immortal."

It's this sort of transcendent insight that we crave, not an affiliation with the author's identity or agenda. We're looking for "a wholeness of being in a narrator that the reader experiences as reliable," as Vivian Gornick observes, "one we can trust will take us on a journey, make the piece arrive, bring us into a clearing where the sense of things is larger than it was before."

ALL OF WHICH SOUNDS JUST DANDY. But what about the realm of fiction, and specifically "unreliable" first-person narrators? Isn't the whole point of such stories that the teller is wickedly inflamed? Well, yes. But if you look at our most famous first-person novels, you'll notice four distinct traits.

First, the narrator is aware that he or she is telling a story. Second, the narrator accepts that it's his or her duty to keep the reader oriented. Third, the narrator offers a clear sense of the book's plot; that is, the tension, conflict, and action to come. And fourth, the narrator is almost inevitably looking back in time, not only to establish greater perspective, but also to differentiate between the character *in* the story and the narrator *telling* the story.

"If you really want to hear about it," Holden Caulfield begins, "the first thing you'll want to know is where I was born, and what my lousy childhood was like, and how my parents were occupied and all before they had me, and all that David Copperfield kind of crap, but I don't feel like going into it, if you want to know the truth. I'll just tell you about this madman stuff that happened to me around last Christmas just before I got pretty run-down and had to come out here and take it easy."

What you hear in this voice is an author striving to establish that strong, independent narrator I keep mentioning. Holden may be young and confused and hurting in ways he's not yet ready to admit, but he's clear about the story he wants to tell us.

When I think about the term "unreliable narrator," the image that leaps to my mind is Wile E. Coyote, who is forever chasing the Road Runner and zooming off various cartoon cliffs. There's always that tense, weirdly poignant moment before Wile E. looks down and plummets into the canyon below. That's how we, as readers, feel, when we're forced to confront the frightening truths our narrator can't.

You will also have noticed that I placed the term *unreliable narrator* in scare quotes. Why? Because human beings are all, in selected moments, unreliable. It depends on when you catch us. Consider the arc of *Flowers for Algernon* by Daniel Keyes. As the story opens, our hero, Charlie Gordon, has an IQ of 68. He doesn't always understand what's happening around him. For instance, he views his coworkers as loyal friends. In fact, they look down on him and mock him behind his back. When research doctors perform an operation that triples his IQ, his perceptions sharpen. Charlie begins to see the world as it really is, including how his doctors regard the mentally disabled as subhuman. Because the story is told through a series of progress reports written by Charlie, we can track how the effects of the surgery recede, and Charlie becomes unreliable again.

MANY OF OUR MOST STRIKING NARRATORS are fundamentally estranged from the world around them. Kazuo Ishiguro's *Klara and the Sun* is narrated by a robot who serves as an "artificial friend" to a dying teenage girl named Josie. Klara is insatiably curious and ravenous to interpret her new surroundings. But she's programmed to view identity as a single value; when people express contradictory emotions—as they are apt to do—her perception of them diffracts. She partitions their feelings into boxes, which she can process only one by one.

It is precisely because Klara doesn't have a human heart that her descriptions of human suffering are so piercing. "Not only was her voice loud," she observes, as she listens to Josie sob for the first time, "it was as if it had been folded over onto itself, so that two versions of her voice were being sounded together, pitched fractionally apart." As we learn more about the excruciatingly engineered world Josie inhabits, the line between organic and inorganic beings blurs. Faced with Josie's impending death, and her own, Klara resorts to the same desperate ploys any human would: pleas, bargains, magical systems of thought.

Klara is a sci-fi variation on the outsider narrator, figures whose isolation acts as a kind of superpower, rendering the familiar as new and strange. This isolation comes in many forms. It could be the psychic break of a teenager such as Holden Caulfield. Or, in the case of Mark Haddon's *The Curious Incident of the Dog in the Night-Time*, a neurodivergent narrator. Christopher Boone tells us that he finds "people confusing." In fact, his ardent struggle to understand those around him—that is, his estrangement—yields astonishing insight: "Sometimes we get sad about things and we don't like to tell other people that we are sad about them. We like to keep it a secret. Or sometimes, we are sad but we really don't know why we are sad, so we say we aren't sad but we really are."

Immigrants represent another category of Outsiders. Consider Jamaica Kincaid's polemic, "On Seeing England for the First Time," in which she writes about the myth of England that shadowed her girlhood in Antigua. "If now as I speak of all this I give the impression of someone on the outside looking in, nose pressed up against a glass window, that is wrong," she notes. "My nose was pressed up against a glass window all right, but there was an iron vise at the back of my neck forcing my head to stay in place."

When Kincaid finally travels to England, as an adult, everything she encounters is polluted by the dark legacy of colonialism: the monuments, erected to mark battles over who "would have dominion over the people who looked like me," the natives whose pale skins "made them look so fragile, so weak, so ugly," even the hedges that carve up the quaint countryside. "I was marveling at all the toil of it," Kincaid writes, "the planting of the hedges to begin with and then the care of it, all that clipping, year after year of clipping, and I wondered at the lives of the people who would have to do this, because wherever I see and feel the hands that hold up the world, I see and feel myself and all the people who look like me." Kincaid's rage is meant not just to raze the lies of the powerful that pass as history, but to illuminate the invisible lives of the oppressed.

In *Wide Sargasso Sea*, Jean Rhys recasts *Jane Eyre* from the perspective of the outsider, Bertha Mason, whose real name is Antoinette. In this telling, noble Mr. Rochester takes possession of his wife's fortune, betrays her, then drags her from Jamaica to England, where he holds her captive. The novel is a chilling parable in which the torching of Thornfield Hall is an act of rebellion against colonial and patriarchal predation. We see Antoinette not as a lunatic but a vulnerable woman abused and gaslit by a monstrous husband.

In her memoir, *Minor Feelings: An Asian American Reckoning*, Cathy Park Hong presents the dynamics of assimilation in a tone that is comic but no less blunt: "Early on, my father learned that in America, one must be emotionally demonstrative to succeed, so he has a habit of saying 'I love you' indiscriminately, to his daughters, to his employees, to his customers, and to airline personnel. He must have observed a salesman affectionately slap another salesman on the back while saying, 'Love ya, man, good to see you!' But because there is no fraternizing man or slap on the back, his usage has an indelicate intimacy, especially since he quietly unloads the endearment as a burning confession: 'Thanks for getting those orders in,' he'll say before hanging up the phone. 'Oh, and Kirby, I love you.'"

Like all outsiders, Hong's powers of observation derive from alienation and its tenant twin, vigilance. As a first-generation Korean American, she is sensitive to the idioms of the dominant culture *and* the immigrant's compulsion to fit in at all costs. As a loyal daughter, she can't help but apprehend the tender and degrading mimicry of her father's sweet talk.

GEORGE ORWELL BELIEVED THAT "the slovenliness of our language makes it easier for us to have foolish thoughts," and that this degradation had clear political effects. I view the erosion of narrative authority in the same way. It's not just a literary dilemma, but a moral disaster. How else should we regard the fact that the most prominent civic narrators of our age—the for-profit demagogues and celebrity politicians—are energetic liars who earn billions spreading inflammatory fictions? Their job is to distract us, both from our private vulnerabilities and the grim data we face as a species.

Literature's mission is just the opposite. Its narrators represent the human capacity to confront truth and find meaning. They activate our imaginations so that we can discover ourselves in the act of reading. We are, in the end, a product of the stories we tell.

In theory, the internet should have granted all of us tremendous narrative power, by providing instant access to an archive of human knowledge and endeavor. In practice, we have used this tool primarily as a hive of distraction, flitting from one context to the next, from Instagram Story to YouTube clip, from ego moment to snarky rant to carnal wormhole.

But the pleasure of writing—and of reading—resides in the capacity to transcend distraction.

I should mention, by way of closing, that I finally got around to watching *Memento*, and that I liked it a lot more than I thought I would. In fact, I saw the movie as a parable of our historical moment.

Leonard Shelby, the amnesiac hero, has been robbed of his identity. He scrawls notes and takes Polaroids to remind himself who he is and what he must do next. Leonard does the work of a narrator: struggling to orient himself, to make sense of his circumstances, to divine the meanings concealed in the baffling world around him. I suspect my students loved *Memento*, in part, because they recognized themselves in his desperate quest. They, too, face a world in disarray, one they yearn to decode. My advice to them remains the same: Do like Leonard. Place your faith in the power of narration.

PART II

SOURCE
MATERIALS

ON THE VARIETIES OF OBSESSION AND ITS NECESSITY AS AN ENGINE OF LITERATURE

'll start with a clarification: this essay will not focus on *writing about the things you love*. When I discuss "obsession," I'll be talking about a feeling state that has clear negative associations, a sense of being stuck, of passion welded to stasis. *Obsess* is one of the few verbs that connotes an internal conflict, all on its own. When I speak of a text as "obsessive," I mean either that its manner of composition (its style) is obsessive or that its plot turns on an obsession. These two often travel together.

Let's proceed from the notion that all readers enter a text with two instinctual questions:

1. Who do I care about?

2. What do they care about?

The sooner these questions are answered, the happier the reader will be. The more inflamed the protagonist's cares are, the deeper our gratification will run. We want from books radical subjectivity. We want feelings that are unstoppable and crazed and shameless precisely because—as we go about the business of responsible living, being dutiful friends and lovers and workers and parents—we are depriving ourselves of these feelings almost constantly. In short, we want obsession: the utter domination of one's thoughts and feelings by a persistent desire, hopefully with calamitous results. That's how sick we are.

A familial case study: Some years ago, my wife, Erin, made some hummus for our extremely discerning four-year-old daughter. In a moment of culinary optimism, Erin sprinkled some paprika onto the hummus. When Josie saw this she reared back.

"What is *that*?" she cried.

Erin smiled gamely. "That's paprika. It's a spice."

"No," Josie shrieked. "No babrika!"

Erin removed the paprika-infested top layer with a spoon, which she placed in my mouth. Five minutes went by.

"Where's the babrika?" Josie wanted to know. "Where does it come from?"

As it would emerge, she wanted all paprika on the earth destroyed (immediately) and the capacity for further production of paprika disabled, with UN inspectors verifying same. The next several days were spent exploring the inexhaustible mysteries of paprika, mysteries I will now, mercifully, spare you.

My point is simple: children are obsessives by nature. Their minds are constantly snagging on potent desires and fears. Part of the reason small children are such voracious readers—aside from the fact that they cannot yet drink—is because they are capable of focusing their attention with such vehemence. So, at the same time I was staring at my daughter in hopeless entreaty, I was also aware that she was taking a literary posture.

If, in fact, we are becoming an increasingly vulgar and reckless species, as the internets have been reporting, the reason is not because we have evolved into unfeeling screen zombies, but because we have surrendered our capacity for sustained attention and the moral imagination that such attention bequeaths. Another way of putting it would be that we've lost the perfectly childish conception of reading as a form of prayer.

Most of the examples I'll cite are drawn from prose. This is not because I have anything against poets. On the contrary, I worship poets for the simple reason that *they will never make any money.* And for the record, I would classify "Song of Myself," "Howl," and Audre Lord's "Coal" as openly, even joyously, obsessive texts.

I'm also going to give short shrift to dramaturgy, though it's obvious that much of Shakespeare springs from obsessive feeling, whether jealousy (*Othello*), ambition (*Macbeth*), or hormonal passions (*Romeo and Juliet*). Eugene O'Neil is a virtual factory of family obsession, Willy Loman is brought low by his obsession with the heroic, even Beckett's most famous play hinges on an obsession with the arrival of Godot.

But my central concern is prose, and so I'll start at or near the beginning, with Don Quixote, whose action is generated by Alonso Quixano's conviction that he must impose chivalric order on the world via the knight errant Don Quixote. Cervantes uses Quixote's obsession to great comic effect. He also makes it perfectly clear that Quixano's alter ego is what keeps him alive. The moment he returns to sanity, at the end of Book Two, he dies—as does the narrative.

Cervantes is among the first novelists to present obsession as a necessary engine of literary enterprise. But you can go ahead and name any classic. Chances are there's a lucrative obsession driving the action. The thrill of *Jane Eyre* resides in the title character's voracious drive to escape the privations of her youth. Subtract Ahab's epic grudge from *Moby-Dick* and you're left with a treatise on the rendering of whale blubber. *Lolita* becomes an episode of *To Catch a Predator* without Humbert Humbert's exquisitely depraved voice.

Humbert is a fine example of what we might call the hypomanic wing of obsessional literature. But it's important to make temperamental distinctions. There are plenty of novels starring repressed heroes who are every bit as besieged by their desires. Take another look at Ishiguro's *The Remains of the Day*. Our narrator, the butler Stevens, is obsessed with dignity, his own and that of his employer, a Nazi sympathizer whom he insists on regarding as a "great man." Stevens is also deeply in love with an ex-colleague and terrified to acknowledge his ardor. His regrets propel the story.

In fact, much of what drives us through a particular story is the unconscious but powerful sense that the narrator *can't* stop obsessing. If the narrator can stop, why should we go on? Aren't we turning to literature in an effort to experience the extreme feeling states of which that responsible life I mentioned earlier so dependably deprives us?

This quality is immediately recognizable in someone such as Vince Thompson, the menacing drug dealer in Keith Lee Morris's novel, *The Dart League King*:

Anyway, the thing to do while waiting for Russell Harmon to reappear was a little fucking reconnaissance, take stock of the situation and formulate a plan, because how did he figure he was going to shoot Russell Harmon anyway on Thursday night at the 321, what with all the stupid ass-holes hanging around, let's see, you had the open mike guy who he could hear at the front of the bar going *testing, testing, fucking testing* and Bill the goddamn bartender and the eight or ten yuppies he'd passed up front on his way in, all real estate agents or builders most likely like practically every other person or so in the whole goddamn town was now, if he was to take his fucking Beretta out on the street at noon on any weekday and start taking potshots with his fucking eyes closed he'd hit a goddamn real estate agent within 7.5 seconds, everyone in town, every lame-brain jerk-ass he'd known for half his life getting their fucking real estate license for money, money, money, *Come build your goddamn mansion on the lake! Piss the whole town to hell, who cares!* so that even if he did find a way to shoot Russell Harmon's ass and get away with it he'd have to drive fucking fifteen miles out of town just to find a decent place to dump his fat ass, whereas twenty years ago he could have practically just dragged his carcass out the back door and dumped it in the goddamn weeds next to Sand Creek and nobody would have found his fucking corpse till Christmas, and when you actually thought about it, it was him, Vince fucking Thompson, who should have been the fucking real estate agent anyway, it was *him* who knew every goddamn square inch of this town, but oh, they'd say, you've gotta get your goddamn license, like you need a fucking license to show someone around a goddamn house, here's the fancy fucking kitchen, here's the goddamn toilet where you piss, you rich California motherfuckers, and oh you've gotta cut your hair, Vince, you've gotta shave more regular and quit carrying a gun around and scaring the shit out of people and acting anti-social and shit, and oh by the way what about that felony conviction and oh by the way would you please piss in this jar. Assholes.

Vince isn't just some gun nut awaiting his *Cops* cameo. He's a sharp guy who can see his hometown succumbing to the great con of gentrification. He knows that he's being left behind and he can't stop dreaming of escape even though he knows he'll never escape. He keeps circling the same story. He is helpless to do otherwise. This is a central dividend of obsessives: one way or another, they admit to everything. And because we would all like to be that fast and loose and brave with the truth, we feel an instinctive gratitude in finally encountering a person immune to our various forms of charm marketing.

I felt the same gratitude the first time I encountered *The Lover* by Marguerite Duras, an autobiographical novella that recalls her precarious childhood as a French girl in colonized Indochina. She writes with ravaging bluntness about the violence and moral lassitude of her debt-stricken family, and the volatile love affair she begins, at age fifteen, with a wealthy Chinese man twice her age.

It is a comfort, she tells us, "to have fallen at last into a misfortune my mother has always predicted for me when she shrieks in the desert of her life." She glories in the racial power she holds over her lover, which, she tells us, started "when he got out of the black car, when he began to approach her, and when she knew, knew he was afraid," and the ecstatic degradations of their coupling ("He becomes rough, desperate, he throws himself on me, devours the childish breasts, shouts, insults. I close my eyes on the intense pleasure").

The perspective shifts between a detached third-person and a first-person confessional, but both are animated by the same force: an obsession that collapses the seventy years between the experiences recalled and the telling of them:

I can't really remember the days. The light of the sun blurred and annihilated all color. But the nights, I remember them. The blue was more distant than the sky, beyond all depths, covering the bounds of the world. The sky, for me, was the stretch of pure brilliance crossing the blue, that cold coalescence beyond all color. Sometimes, it was in Vinh Long, when my mother was sad she'd order the gig and we'd drive out into the country to see the night as it was in the dry season. I had that good fortune—those nights, that mother. The light fell from the sky in cataracts of pure transparency, in torrents of silence and immobility. The air was blue, you could hold it in your hand. Blue. The sky was the continual throbbing of the brilliance of the light. The night lit up everything, all the country on either bank of the river as far as the eye could reach. Every night was different, each one had a name as long as it lasted. Their sound was that of the dogs, the country dogs baying at mystery. They answered one another from village to village, until the time and space of the night were utterly consumed.

That's the essence of obsession: utter consumption.

As a literary substrate, this certainly sounds lucrative. But the real-time experience, for the writer, is a disorderly rush of thought and feeling and detail. Sentences like the ones Morris and Duras craft are deceptively hard to write. They mimic thought, a dense and associative process. In the wrong hands, such efforts can become hopelessly mangled. Worse, they can begin to reflect the author's infatuations with language, rather than the character's preoccupations. This is a fair summary of the mindset that generated my first two novels, which I will now do you the great kindness of not quoting.

The other risk is technical and impossible to avoid: an obsessive text is, by its nature, hopelessly biased, and this bias comes at the cost of perspective. We are left without a reliable guide. This, I suspect, is why so many novels about obsessives are written by secondary characters—see: *The Bluest Eye*, *My Brilliant Friend*, *Gatsby*, etc.—who are capable of sympathizing with the afflicted while offering the insight that comes with distance.

An obsessive narrator generates tension simply by holding forth. Because, as noted, we are always telling two stories about ourselves: the one about who we want to believe we are, and the one about who we know ourselves to be. Nearly all the humiliating events in our lives (and much of the best prose) can be said to arise from the collision of these two stories.

With an obsessive narrator, the author's role is not to protect or malign the accused. The goal is simply to transcribe those outbursts that offer us the greatest insight into our hero's psyche. This needn't be a litany of family secrets and primal urges. In *The Mezzanine*, Nicholson Baker wrings pathos from the obsessive musings of his hero over such matters as straw technology and shoelaces. What matters isn't the object but the ardor.

The same dynamics prevail in short stories. One of my recent favorites, "Girls, at Play" by Celeste Ng, focuses on a pack of working-class teenage girls who seek power by submitting to a sexual game with boys on the playground. When a new girl, Grace, appears at school, they absorb her into their clique and cling to her innocence, even as they verse her in the arts of self-exploitation. The story culminates with the girls teaching Grace the game—an initiation rite that reads like a sexual assault. In corrupting Grace, the girls relinquish their own childhoods.

It's a story—much like Edgar Allan Poe's agitated monologues—driven by obsessive guilt. The same can be said of Frank O'Connor's "Guests of the Nation": an aging war veteran cannot banish the memory of having executed two prisoners of war who became his friends. The story is a ramp that leads, inexorably, to those killings. Your job, especially in short fiction, is to find those moments that your protagonists cannot banish by other means.

In turning to nonfiction, I want to offer an amuse-bouche—Calvin Trillin from his delicious volume *Feeding a Yen*:

No, I do not believe it's fair to say that for the past fifteen years I've thought of nothing but the fried fish I once ate on Baxters Road. That statement would be inaccurate even if you expanded it to include the chicken, also fried, that I ate on Baxters Road at around the same time.

With a single sentence, Trillin manages to answer those two questions—*Who do we care about? What do they care about?*—while also conveying a lot about his character: that he's mildly ashamed of his obsession and attractively helpless to fight it. Trillin doesn't clear his throat. He writes *into* his obsessions, not around them.

Joan Didion does the same thing, though more cerebrally, in "Goodbye to All That":

It is easy to see the beginnings of things, and harder to see the ends. I can remember now, with a clarity that makes the nerves in the back of my neck constrict, when New York began for me, but I cannot lay my finger upon the moment it ended, can never cut through the ambiguities and second starts and broken resolves to the exact place on the page where the heroine is no longer as optimistic as she once was.

Notice the title, which tells us the piece is written in the retrospective voice. Didion is looking back on the years she spent in New York. You can safely assume that if you are consciously obsessed with something *right now*, you're going to have trouble writing about it well. Why? Because its full significance has not yet become clear to you. And because you yourself, as you currently exist, are not yet clear to you.

Didion's essay is an elegant compendium of *moments* from her New York years, the moments she has been unable to forget. These are not the expected landmarks—her first big break, or heartbreak—but quieter episodes that have come to symbolize the experience: the exaltation of eating a peach on Lexington Avenue at twilight; the dejection of watching "the long panels of transparent golden silk" hung in her window become "tangled and drenched in afternoon thunderstorms."

I am constantly imploring students to pay special attention to anything they can't forget. If an image, or interaction, or sensation, or snatch of dialogue snags in your consciousness, it bears investigation.

This applies to relationships, too. In the memoir *Stay True*, Hua Hsu recounts the bond he forged twenty-five years ago, as a freshman at Berkeley, with Ken, whose genial frat-boy conformity clashes with Hsu's straight-edge rebellion. Their intense bond ends in a shocking tragedy; a carjacker kills Ken. It's not the murder that matters here, but the author's tender determination to commemorate his friend and to understand their unlikely friendship.

The book becomes a quietly revelatory exploration of how we construct identity. "When you're young," Hsu observes, "you do so many things hoping to be noticed. The way you dress or stand, the music played loud enough to catch the attention of another person who might know a song, too." Ken is the one person who notices the wounded need for affirmation roiling beneath Hsu's sneering façade.

Sometimes, of course, our obsessions crush us into silence. This is certainly the case for Natasha Trethewey. It took her more than three decades to write the aforementioned *Memorial Drive*. The book chronicles Trethewey's childhood, as the daughter of a mixed-race couple in the South, then proceeds, with grim determination, toward the murder of her mother by her stepfather—a story she's stifled for years. "When I finally sit down to write the part of our story I've most needed to avoid," Trethewey observes, "when I force myself at last to read the evidence, all of it—the transcripts, witness accounts, the autopsy and officials reports, the [prosecutor's] statement, indications of police indifference—I collapse on the floor, keening as though I had just learned of my mother's death."

We resist writing about our obsessions because we fear the psychic disruption of *utter consumption*. And also because our obsessions come spring-loaded with shame. In "A Few Words About Breasts," Nora Ephron cops to a lifelong obsession with having a flat chest, which she traces back to the crushing gender conformity of the 1950s. "I did not feel at all like a girl. I was athletic, ambitious, outspoken, competitive, noisy, rambunctious," she explains. "I wanted desperately not to be that way, not to be a mixture of both things, but instead just one, a girl, a definite indisputable girl. As soft and as pink as a nursery. And nothing would do that for me, I felt, but breasts."

This is how it works with obsessions. They develop to satisfy psychic and spiritual needs, not just to fill our minds and hearts with junk. There is no such thing as a meaningless obsession, because obsession itself is the deepest form of human meaning.

Nick Hornby affirms this in his memoir, *Fever Pitch*. It focuses on his worship of the British soccer team Arsenal, which infiltrates his thoughts within minutes of waking *every single morning*. I had never even heard of Arsenal before I picked up the book. As I read, I began to feel Hornby's allegiance taking root inside me. In recounting his obsession, Hornby relates the story of his own childhood, his loneliness, his search for a connection with his father, and a place in the world of men.

I should admit at this point that I spent many years, early in my writing career, keeping my obsessions out of my creative life—at least consciously. Writing about them too directly felt like a cheat, as if I were dodging the deeper imaginative and symbolic work required of a True Writer. But a pattern began to develop. I would endure the failure of some grand literary project, usually a novel, and find myself blocked. At which point I would turn to one of my obsessions (candy, football, politics) as a path back to the keyboard. Pieces born as newspaper stories or short essays would start to expand, evolve, deepen, and widen in scope, until I realized—often to my own bemusement—that they were books.

I say bemusement because the writing came so quickly and easily. But of course it did; I'd been harboring these obsessions for decades. My mind was stuffed with memories, associations, facts, and insights, and I was wildly curious to conduct additional research. My friends and family were often surprised to read these books, because I had so carefully hidden my obsessions from view.

The books themselves invariably turned in directions I wasn't expecting. In chronicling my addiction to football (*Against Football*), I wound up exploring the toxic masculinity of my family, the ways insecurity and violence interact, and my own weakness for tribal adoration. My candy memoir (*Candyfreak*) was actually a book about all the ways we seek a path away from our despair. The most exciting part of any obsession is the part you don't yet understand. Tracking your obsession should lead you into mystery and reveal things about you that you don't want revealed. Your job is to peer into the dark regions of your heart, not navel gaze.

I truly believe that anyone who writes about those things that matter to them most deeply—whether by means of fiction or nonfiction—and who does so in a genuine effort to reveal truth, will find an audience. At the very least they will feel unburdened of the glorious secret of who they really are.

FREE WRITE

Think about the most persistent obsession you had as a kid. Doesn't matter what it was—a toy, a TV show, a kind of food, a band, a brand of cereal. Your job is to tell us about that obsession, how it took root, what pleasures (or terrors) it yielded, the rituals and relics that obtained around it. What memories leap to mind? At some point, you may want to step back and tell us about what else was going on in your life, as that's probably relevant. Hint: Whichever obsession feels the most embarrassing to admit, that's the one that's most alive and most deserving of your literary attention.

CRUSHING IT

DESIRE PLACED IN PERIL = STORY

As a high-volume teacher of workshops (i.e., a glorified adjunct who has to hustle to pay the bills), I'm lucky enough to see a wide sampling of the stories being written these days. Most of them feature vivid language, compelling characters, and ambitious themes. There is one crucial area, however, where they consistently fall short of their potential: the stories suffer from emotional cowardice.

Cowardice is a loaded word. I could soften it up if you like. I could say emotive timidity. Or fecklessness. But what I mean here is something closer to a failure of will.

Time and again, I am presented with stories in which the author has placed her protagonist in some variety of crisis. They are betrayed by a shitty lover, exploited by a cruel parent, cast out from the family of man. And yet these stories, having engineered such disequilibrium, are reluctant to engage with the full human measure of what these people are suffering. Too often, the emotional violence of the story is held in check, teased at, outright evaded, or channeled into defensive emotions.

We offer dents in the characters' defensive armor, or a fleeting glimpse of the welts beneath. It's not enough. Our characters must dream and must have those dreams assaulted, must suffer what the essayist Sarah Manguso calls "the burden of hope." We need to stop protecting our characters (and ourselves) from the very thing our reader has arrived most eager to experience: uncontainable emotion.

I am not calling for opera. I'm advocating for passages that result from an author carefully and methodically building a ramp to an unforgettable moment, then *slowing down*. It's what happens when your heroine is overrun by feeling and you, the author, refuse to look away. You face their anguish and your own deepest intention.

As intimate as a writing workshop can appear, we are generally not equipped to talk about this stuff. It feels too personal, too squishy, too *therapeutic*. We feel safer debating craft, point of view, narrative strategy, the polite dogmas and counterdogmas of our given racket. The real question is this: What does your heroine desire? What stands in her way? Allow a character to yearn, and you make them vulnerable. Force them to shoulder the burden of hope, and we will follow them anywhere.

Love is a smoke made with the fume of sighs. That's how Shakespeare puts it in the first scene of *Romeo and Juliet*. It's useful to recall how that play begins. Romeo, mooning over some lesser Capulet, catches sight of Juliet at her family's ball and, after a little digital frottage, falls hard. Tybalt is then barely restrained from killing Romeo.

The pragmatists among us are inclined to recommend that Romeo look for a lover less likely to get him disemboweled. But we don't look to literature for pragmatism. In fact, I'd argue that Romeo and Juliet are turned on by the revelation that their kin are sworn enemies, which must appeal to the histrionic masochism that is a central feature of adolescence.

Consider the saga of Heathcliff and Catherine, two crazy kids who roam the moors of Wuthering Heights pining for each other but never quite consummating. What's the problem? They are born of different classes. Also, Heathcliff is kind of a jerk. But man do they yearn:

> Be with me always—take any form—drive me mad! Only do not leave me in this abyss, where I cannot find you! Oh, God! it is unutterable! I can not live without my life! I can not live without my soul! . . .
>
> I have to remind myself to breathe—almost to remind my heart to beat!

Stripped of their context, these declarations sound overheated and frankly juvenile. They call to mind a conversation I had once with one of my students. I was imploring her to stop worrying about her prose and instead to focus on the volcanic lust and loneliness lurking within her leading man. "The thing about emotion," she told me, "is that I'm afraid I'll wind up sounding like a thirteen-year-old girl writing in her journal."

She meant mushy, sentimental.

I get it. I've heard dozens of students voice the same anxiety. What I think they're expressing, in most cases, is an aversion to the dangers of deep feeling. After all, in our civilian lives, we are constantly seeking to *avoid* drama. We dodge conflict. We hold

our desire in check. When confronted by our darkest fears—that
we are unworthy of love, for instance—we seek the false light of
denial, distraction, rationalization. Is it any wonder that so many
of our characters do the same thing?

To be clear: Sentiment isn't emotion. It's *false* emotion. More
precisely, emotion that's asserted by the writer, rather than experienced by the characters.

But doesn't yearning—if we truly face it—make us all sort of
adolescent? Isn't the whole point that we are remitted to that
glorious capital city of angst? Here's how Toni Morrison
describes the onset of love in *Sula*:

> They ran in the sunlight, creating their own breeze which
> pressed their dresses into their damp skin. Reaching a kind
> of square of four locked trees which promised cooling; they
> flung themselves into the shade to taste their lip sweat and
> contemplate the wildness that had come upon them so
> suddenly.

Yes.

Here's Nick Carraway channeling his doomed pal Gatsby:

> His heart beat faster and faster as Daisy's white face came
> up to his own. He knew that when he kissed this girl, and
> forever wed his unutterable visions to her perishable
> breath, his mind would never romp again like the mind of
> God. So he waited, listening for a moment longer to the
> tuning fork that had been struck upon a star. Then he

kissed her. At his lips' touch she blossomed like a flower and the incarnation was complete.

There must have been moments even that afternoon when Daisy tumbled short of his dreams—not through her own fault, but because of the colossal vitality of his illusion. It had gone beyond her, beyond everything. He had thrown himself into it with a creative passion, adding to it all the time, decking it out with every bright feather that drifted his way. No amount of fire or freshness can challenge what a man will store up in his ghostly heart.

Is that mushy? Or is that the "burden of hope"? Aren't stories intended to unburden us of what we store up in our ghostly hearts?

This is the one area where fiction faces a greater challenge than nonfiction. In the world of nonfiction, we are damned to tell stories from the life we've led, one in which inhibition often trumps desire. In fiction, it is our duty to engineer the plot so as to slam our characters up against their desires. Readers arrive hoping for vicarious forms of ruin.

Sarah Manguso tells this story in her brilliant book of micro-essays, *300 Arguments*: "In ninth grade I was too afraid to speak to the boy I loved, so I mailed him a black paper heart every week for a year. I wasn't afraid of him; I was afraid of my feeling. It was more powerful than God. If we'd ever spoken it might have burned the whole place down."

It's no accident that Manguso is writing about a crush, because the crush is the relational prototype of desire placed in peril. It's Want dashed against the rocks of Not Going to Happen; love transmuted into self-punishment. Crushes have a miraculous staying power precisely because they remain undiluted by the inevitable letdowns of fulfillment. They endure as repositories of our fantasy life, a realm where a few muzzy details, nourished by the imagination, can seize our attention for months at a time.

In our work as writers, attention represents the basic unit of measurement. We recall moments from childhood and adolescence more vividly than recent ones because we were paying attention more purely. This is especially true of the infatuations that took root before we had a chance to fortify our defenses, to hedge our emotional bets.

When it comes to crushes, we memorize every smile, every word, every freckle. We search for relics and clues. We caress the places warmed by their bodies. We sniff the air for a trace of their scent. We measure our days by our hopes of seeing them. And because we give them so much of ourselves—our attention, our desire, our love—the reader cannot help but feel it. Crushes activate desires we cannot control; we give ourselves over to them without restraint. Our readers deserve the same courage.

Hell, so do we.

FREE WRITE

Please write about your most devout, ecstatic, humiliating crush from childhood or adolescence. Orient us with a little context (how old you were, where this took place), then describe your crush: how they looked, moved, smelled, whatever you can still remember. Tell us about how you felt in their presence, and any rituals that presided as you sought proximity to them. Was this crush ever confessed to, or consummated? What was going on in the rest of your life? Looking back, were there aspects of your crush that you envied, or coveted, that you wished to possess for yourself? This needn't be a purely romantic crush. It could be a friend crush, a crush on an inappropriate figure, such as a teacher or older cousin, or even a fantasy crush on a rock star. It could be on a crush on a fictional character, such as Harry Potter. Please don't aim for fancy prose. Just go back there and help us feel what you felt. Consider this a radical experiment in facing your emotional intention.

FUNNY IS THE NEW DEEP

AN EXPLORATION OF THE COMIC IMPULSE

Most people's formal introduction to what I'll be calling "the comic impulse" arrives via Aristotle. Yes, him again.

In the *Poetics*, Aristotle writes about four literary modes: the tragic, epic, lyric, and comic. This taxonomy has led to a vague consensus that the tragic and comic modes of literature are distinct and diametrically opposed. This notion is, to apply the ancient Greek term, *bullshiz*. The comic impulse arises directly from our efforts to contend with tragedy. It is the safest and most effective way to acknowledge our circumstances without being crushed by them.

Writers early in their careers tend to look down upon the comic impulse. I certainly did. Back in the mid-nineties, when I was excreting my initial drafts, I wanted more than anything to be taken *seriously*. If enough people took me seriously, then I might start to take myself seriously, thereby dispelling the notion, forever lurking at the gates of ambition, that I was a sad clown who should quit writing and return to my given career as the world's most inept investigative reporter. Big awards, and the vengeful omnipotence that came with them, went to folks like Hemingway and Faulkner, who did not smile, let alone crack wise.

This mindset led to the production of many earnest and dreary pieces of short fiction intended to prove my good habits of thought and feeling. I really was a nice Jewish boy from the suburbs, clean, obedient, *serious*.

To me, back then, perhaps as to you, here and now, the "comic impulse" meant a conscious desire to be funny, to entertain people, to make them laugh. As a practical matter, the absolute worst way to pursue a career in the comic arts is to try to be funny. It doesn't work that way. Comedy is produced by a determined confrontation with a set of feeling states that are tragic in nature: grief, shame, disappointment, physical discomfort, anxiety, moral outrage. Forget pleasing the crowd. Purge thyself.

Comedy is rooted in this capacity to face painful truths and to offer, by means of laughter, a dividend of forgiveness. I learned this from Lorrie Moore, among others. As a novice story writer, I studied her collection *Birds of America* like a holy text. How was she able to write so uproariously about characters who were plainly depressed and adrift? Here's the actress Sidra, from "Willing":

> And so she left Hollywood. Phoned her agent and apologized. Went home to Chicago, rented a room by the week at the Days Inn, drank sherry, and grew a little plump. She let her life get dull—dull, but with Hostess cakes. There were moments bristling with deadness, when she looked out at her life and went "What?" Or worse, feeling interrupted and tired, "Wha—?" It had taken on

the shape of a terrible mistake. She hadn't been given the proper tools to make a real life with, she decided, that was it. She'd been given a can of gravy and a hairbrush and told, "There you go." She'd stood there for years, blinking and befuddled, brushing the can with the brush.

Mein Gott! I must have read this passage a thousand times. Moore was fearless in tracking her heroine's shame spiral yet never downcast or judgmental. We got the squalid details (Days Inn, sherry) but also the treats ("dull, but with Hostess cakes"), the torpor and confusion, but also the strange, enchanting associations. Sidra had hit bottom, but she still felt pleasure, still imagined, still struggled to divine the roots of her dilemma. This is how the reader could tell she still felt hope. There was mercy in her jokes.

The comic impulse is simultaneously an expression of helplessness, of surrender to the world's absurd cruelty, and our own foibles and fuckups, *and*, at the same time, the acquisition of power by means of acknowledging that bad data.

Kurt Vonnegut, my first literary hero, performed this feat in all his novels. I assumed Vonnegut had come to the page a supreme wiseass. But when I went to examine his papers twenty years ago, I discovered something shocking: as a young writer, Vonnegut wanted ardently to be taken . . . *seriously*. He had returned home from World War II determined to capture the gravity of what he had witnessed, in particular the firebombing of Dresden. Vonnegut wrote dozens of short stories. Terse, competent, lifeless stories. My sole reward for slogging through them was the revelation that Kurt Vonnegut's prose once sucked.

These stories contained many of the events and characters that would later appear in his masterpiece, *Slaughterhouse-Five*. If you read the introduction to that novel, what you hear is surrender—to the human capacity for cruelty, of course, but also to his own literary inadequacies:

> I would hate to tell you what this lousy little book cost me in money and anxiety and time. When I got home from the Second World War twenty-three years ago, I thought it would be easy for me to write about the destruction of Dresden, since all I would have to do would be to report what I had seen. And I thought, too, that it would be a masterpiece or at least make me a lot of money, since the subject was so big.
>
> But not many words about Dresden came from my mind then—not enough of them to make a book, anyway. And not many words come now, either, when I have become an old fart with his memories and his Pall Malls, with his sons full grown.

The most fascinating document in the entire Vonnegut archive is the letter he wrote to his family on May 29, 1945, from a repatriation camp in Le Havre, France, days after he'd been liberated: "I'm told that you were probably never informed that I was anything other than 'missing in action,'" he begins. "That leaves me a lot of explaining to do ... On about Feb. 14 the Americans came over, follow by the RAF. Their combined labors killed [25,000] people in 24 hours and destroyed all of Dresden—possibly the world's most beautiful city. But not me."

That is Vonnegut's voice, that fearless surrender to the absurd. It was inside of him all that time. And it's inside of you, too. Every single person on earth, and thus every writer, has a distinct sense of humor. It's what we use to survive our families, our heartbreaks, the all-purpose hell of adolescence. We laugh to keep from wallowing.

The comic impulse, it turns out, isn't a literary device at all. It's a bio-evolutionary adaptation. It's the survival tool human beings developed to contend with the burdens of self-consciousness and moral awareness, as well as the horrible outcomes they needed to imagine to survive as a prey species roaming the Serengeti, or the Neander Valley.

It's also the tool we've relied on to confront moral atrocities of our own making. This is the tradition that connects the satires of Aristophanes to the barbs of *The Daily Show*. Witness *King Lear*: the only character allowed to straight talk the king is the fool. Why? Because he drapes his moral critique in a cloak of laughter. Charlie Chaplin did the same thing. In 1940, with America and Britain formally at peace with Nazi Germany, he made *The Great Dictator*, a comedy that portrayed Nazis, quite literally, as killing machines.

Which brings us back to Vonnegut and *Slaughterhouse-Five*, one of two great American novels to emerge from the cataclysm of World War II. The other? *Catch-22* by Joseph Heller.

The comic impulse is what we use to predict ruin and reckon with it. Am I suggesting that atrocity is the midwife of the funny? That, without the abomination of slavery, Mark Twain never writes *Huckleberry Finn*? Yeah, I am. And actually, I'm saying the opposite, too. The comic impulse allows us to confront our sins (personal, cultural, historical) and thereby make moral progress. It does so by granting us a license to traffic in the transgressive.

A prime example is Paul Beatty's audacious novel *The Sellout*, in which our hero, Bonbon, attempts to revitalize his hometown by reinstituting segregation and slavery, going so far as to take legal possession of a slave himself. Bonbon, it bears mentioning, is African American, as are most of his fellow residents.

Reading *The Sellout*, one hears the echo of Jonathan Swift's *A Modest Proposal*, which opens with a lamentation for the Irish poor before proceeding to an ingenious solution: peddling its offspring to the British as a delicacy. ("A young healthy child well nursed, is, at a year old, a most delicious nourishing and wholesome food, whether stewed, roasted, baked, or boiled; and I make no doubt that it will equally serve in a fricassee, or a ragout.")

Swift targets the pious cruelty of the colonizer; Beatty assaults the myth of a post-racial America when our entire economic system is predicated on white supremacy. The comic impulse in these works is a force of radicalism, in which writers embrace taboos to confront inconvenient truths.

But this confrontation need not be with corrosive systems of power. More often, in literature, the enemy is within. The comic impulse, in such cases, fuels the articulation of private, forbidden thoughts. Consider how Philip Roth leaped from the gentle satire of *Goodbye, Columbus* to the libidinal outpouring of *Portnoy's Complaint*.

The novels of Austen, or the comedies of Shakespeare, though refined in manner, glory in the brutal exposure of vanities, delusions, and prejudices. There's a long tradition of comic novels driven by misfits whose bumbling quests (for love, for justice, for decent employment) reveal their own flaws and lay waste to those around them. Don Quixote begets Tristram Shandy who begets Ignatius J. Reilly, Bridget Jones, Bernadette Fox, Oscar Wao, Arthur Less.

Which of these novels you will enjoy depends on your comic sensibility. When I was in high school, there were (and, I suspect, still are) a loyal troupe of kids who spent hours reenacting the skits of Monty Python. There were others who lit their farts on fire. And still others who devoured Wodehouse.

This sensibility is not static. As a six-year-old, I had to be forcibly removed from a local theater by my mother because I had gone into uncontrollable hysterics during a Marx Brothers film. A few years later, I would embrace the juvenile snark of *Mad Magazine* and, still later, the stoned picaresque of the underground comic *The Fabulous Furry Freak Brothers*.

To me, the comic impulse is a nontransferable asset. You can't convince someone that a joke or a movie or a book is, or isn't, funny. But I will say a few things that I think apply across the board. Something is funny, most of all, because it's true, and because the velocity of insight as to this truth exceeds our normal standards.

Exhibit A: "The Wisdom of Children" a short piece by Simon Rich that adorned my fridge for more than a decade. It takes the form of a conversation at the grown-up table, as envisioned at the kids' table:

MOM: Pass the wine, please. I want to become crazy.
DAD: O.K. . . .

MOM: I'm angry! I'm angry all of a sudden!
DAD: I'm angry, too! We're angry at each other!
MOM: Now everything is fine.

These five lines of imagined dialogue rocket us through the emotional arc of alcoholism, marital strife, and fraudulent reconciliation.

I feel the same bolt of gratification when an essayist such as Samantha Irby annihilates the self-destructive drama we mistake for love, as she does in "I'm in Love and It's Boring" from her collection *We Are Never Meeting in Real Life*:

> Real love feels less like a throbbing, pulsing animal begging for its freedom and beating against the inside of my chest and more like, 'Hey, that place you like had fish tacos today and i got you some while i was out,' as it sets a bag spotted with grease on the dining room table. It's not a game you don't understand the rules of, or a test you never got the materials to study for. It never leaves you wondering who could possibly be texting at 3 am. Or what you could possibly do to make it come home and stay there. It's fucking boring, dude. I don't walk around mired in uneasiness, waiting for the other shoe to drop. No parsing through spun tales about why it took her so long to come back from the store. No checking her emails or calling her job to make sure she's actually there. No sitting in my car outside her house at dawn, to make sure she's alone when she leaves. This feels safe, and steadfast, and predictable. And secure. It's boring as shit. And it's easily the best thing I've ever felt.

When I first read this, I felt thankful a writer had articulated, so plainly, something I've struggled to grasp for years: that love comes down to consideration, reliability, trust. What makes the passage funny is the path Irby takes to this truth, through the torments of her previous relationships, which she delineates without a hint of grievance or self-pity. Her tone is one of exhausted relief. (*It's fucking boring, dude.*) She's not triumphant about her newfound equanimity; she's stupefied by it.

What else?

Something is funny because it's outside our accepted boundary of decorum. Something is funny because it defies our expectations. Something is funny because it offers a temporary reprieve from the hardship of seeing the world as it actually is, or because we are offered a shocking clarity as to the true nature of our lives. There are different sorts of laughter, and they express varying degrees of delight, affirmation, surprise, relief, and mercy.

It's possible at this point that I've made the comic impulse sound like some kind of moral disinfectant, so let's add a few putrid adjectives to that list: contempt, cruelty, complicity. Call it the laughter of the troll: that nervous titter when a demagogue imitates a disabled person or mocks victims of sexual assault. Or when an author, striving to charm the reader, mocks his characters, or indulges in lazy generalizations.

Am I judging laughter here? Yeah, I am. As a species, we're complex and variable, capable of laughing at others in ways that are demeaning and selfish. That's not the comedy that endures. The comedy that endures challenges us to laugh at ourselves, to recognize and accept our own weakness.

The goal isn't to crack jokes but to engage in a ruthless pursuit of the truth. David Sedaris, the foremost humorist of our age, has become funnier in direct proportion to the darkness of his concerns. He used to write about dressing up as a Christmas elf. These days, he writes about death, alcoholism, suicide.

The comic impulse isn't some wrench you hoist out of your writer's toolbox when the action flags. It's what arises when you reach a moment that is too painful to confront without some form of self-forgiveness. It's not a conscious decision, but an unconscious necessity.

I keep thinking here about an undergraduate I taught two decades ago, Tracey Wigfield. Tracey wore preppy clothes and didn't say much in class. Occasionally, though, she would uncork some exquisitely wry and piercing observation. I saw something of myself in Tracey, the young striver determined to be taken seriously and therefore inhibiting her comic powers.

This was, of course, total bullshit. Tracey was already an aspiring humorist. She just happened to be a subtle person who didn't feel the need—like some people I could mention—to show off constantly. Also, the class was about cultural critique and most of the readings I assigned were hopelessly serious.

Anyway, during office hours, I told Tracey that her sense of humor could inform her cultural critiques, something she almost certainly already knew. Her final piece for class was a press conference delivered by Barbie, the doll. It was a droll and subversive send-up of celebrity culture and self-commodification, and so funny that I read it to my wife.

Years later, I received a handwritten note from Tracey, thanking me for encouraging her. She added that she was now one of

100

the lead writers for the television show *30 Rock*. I had two rapid-fire reactions to this note:

1. My God, how incredible and inspiring!

2. I am now going to kill myself.

But look: Tracey was the kind of person who needed the comic impulse to fully liberate herself as a writer. It was how she operated off the page as well.

I'm stressing this because I continue to encounter students who tell me they want to "make" their stories funnier, or that they need to "put some humor" in them. Such efforts are doomed for the simple reason that they represent the author's need for adulation. It's like when someone races up to you and says, "Omigod, listen to this joke! It's hilarious!" Not anymore.

Remember, your sense of humor did not begin as a narrative strategy but as an adaptive instinct. That's what it should remain in your work. The idea is not to hide behind a set of jokes, but to relax sufficiently so as to allow for some play, some improvisation, at the keyboard.

In revision, the question is simple: Does the funny line help my characters face the truth of their circumstance? Or does it distract from that truth? (I should mention here that I cut not one but *two* vulgar jokes while revising this piece, on the advice of my editor, whose sense of humor does not quite extend to my autoerotic habits.)

I'm thinking now about the first humor writing class I ever taught. I assumed it would be a cinch, because college students constantly talk shit to each other. All I had to do was get them to talk shit onto the page.

But these were Boston College undergraduates who, like me, regarded writing as a battle for respectability. They kept turning in earnest satires meant to condemn the horrors of racism, sexism, and the like. A month into class, I convened a come-to-Jesus meeting. "Listen," I said. "I love you guys, but you're playing it way too safe. If I receive another obedient word in this class, so help me God, I will flunk every one of you. I can do that. I'm an adjunct."

The next class, this kid Pete brought in a piece on pooping in public. It was a long and detailed primer that introduced the reader to terms such as *the half-crap* and *prairie-dogging*. Wow. That class was an excruciating and deeply awesome fifty minutes of life. The piece was so extreme, and so courageous in confronting the most private of our shared shames, that it broke the class wide open.

The real question isn't whether you can or should try to be funny in your work, but whether you're going to get yourself and your characters into enough danger to invoke the comic impulse. Funny writers want you to laugh. But they want you to laugh so you can apprehend and endure the astonishing sorrow of the examined life.

FREE WRITE

OK, folks, it's time to acknowledge your own shit!
Please think about an episode of physical humiliation in your life. A moment, hypothetically, in
which, for instance, you farted audibly during a high
school play, specifically during a moment of tremendous and dramatic silence onstage, so that everyone
in the audience, including your crush, Kendall
Gilmore, who was sitting in the row right behind
you, looking feathered and beautiful, knew that it
was you who farted, and you had to sit for the next
minute or so, as the rotten-egg stink of that fart—
which, again, had just loudly exited your ass—slowly
seeped into the nostrils of everyone within a
twenty-foot radius, very much including Kendall, and
how everyone had to pretend that it wasn't happening, most especially you, and how later, after the play,
you were walking across the parking lot and you
could hear Kendall and all her friends laughing
uproariously until they spotted you and fell into a
hushed silence.

Reminder: This example is so completely non-autobiographical it's not even funny.

Some pro tips for your free write . . .

PRO TIP #1: There is some chance you have told this story before, though probably it was at a loud party and you were drunk.

PRO TIP #2: You are not trying to be funny here. You are trying to tell the truth about this particular moment of awfulness, and trying, at the same time, to be forgiving of the person who was experiencing it (i.e., younger you).

PRO TIP #3: While, at the same time, slowing down to examine everything that made the moment so particularly awful, such as the fact, in our non-autobiographical example, that the play during which you farted was actually about a veteran who had been wounded in some distant war, and how the very handsome actor who was playing that veteran, a senior who Kendall Gilmore, now that you think about it, was probably fucking, or very much wanted to fuck, was delivering the play's culminating monologue, a monologue studded with long, actorly pauses, one of which your digestive system involuntarily punctuated, and how that gust of flatulence was no doubt gossiped about for weeks and perhaps even months afterward, with everyone present telling all of their friends how disgusting the smell was and not one of those people pausing to consider how possibly depraved it was that our high school was staging a play about a young man maimed in battle rather than, say, *Our Town*, or goddamn *Oklahoma!*

PRO TIP #4: Have fun.

RUN HOWLING
TOWARD THE DOUBT

O h, to be a writer in this age of apocalyptic tech. Just look around the subway. People used to read books! Now they've got their noses pressed to tiny screens, mainlining *Love Is Blind* and *Candy Crush*. If that weren't depressing enough, now comes ChatGPT to put us all out of business for good.

Only: no. Knock it off. Artificial intelligence programs pose no threat to your work as a writer. Bots do not possess a mind or heart or soul. They do not dream up stories. They generate content—mindlessly, heartlessly, soullessly—by looking for patterns in huge troves of language and predicting the next word.

Practically speaking, this is the precise opposite of how writers work. We're looking for language that is *unexpected*—unexpectedly precise, unexpectedly nuanced, unexpectedly musical—language that arises not from an algorithm combing a random universe of text but from our inimitable relationship to the language, formed by the particular vernaculars and sympathies we grew up absorbing.

AI language programs mimic. They don't create. Ask one to compose a sonnet and it will spit out fourteen lines of doggerel. That's not a person making word decisions. It's a machine performing a task.

Much has been made of the eerily "human" conversations such programs have generated. For instance, the philosopher Seth Lazar goaded Bing's chatbot into typing, "I can blackmail you, I can threaten you, I can hack you, I can expose you, I can ruin you," which is, parenthetically, the exact text message Vladimir Putin sends Donald Trump every night, just before the two of them retire to their caskets. *New York Times* tech columnist Kevin Roose spent hours prodding a bot and elicited ardent declarations of love that shaded into menace. Roose said he had trouble sleeping afterward.

So what happened next?

In Lazar's case, the bot—recognizing it had violated its parameters—immediately erased its threatening messages. In Roose's case, Bing's PR staff rushed to reassure the world that they had fixed the bugs that caused their chatbot to go rogue. In other words, these "human-seeming" reactions were treated as defects.

I hope you can see the profoundly anti-literary outlook on display here. A central goal of literature, if not *the* central goal, is to express the disruptive feelings we spend the rest of our lives trying to muzzle. We write stories in the explicit *hope* that our readers will have trouble sleeping afterward.

A simpler way of saying all this is that chatbots are programmed to combat doubt. They want to answer your questions and fulfill your wishes. Writers want just the opposite: to engage in productive bewilderment.

"WE LIVE WITH MYSTERY, but we don't like the feeling. I think we should get used to it." That's how the poet Mark Strand describes the situation.

I never met Strand, though I saw him read back in 1999. That was the year I spent making deliriously bad poetry. I didn't realize how bad it was at the time, obviously. I knew only that prose had become an insufficient vehicle for my genius; this was why my short stories kept getting rejected. I needed to rip the language open and sing.

I was depressed, of course, painfully lonely, scrambling between adjunct gigs in a pale green Tercel, whose rusted undercarriage would eventually shed a wheel in traffic. Every Thursday, I drove to the Cantab Lounge and abused the open mic. I haunted local readings, vibrating with angst and stabbing insights onto a napkin because I couldn't be bothered to buy a notebook. At one point, I organized an evening of verse, with professional poets, and—in a harrowing act of self-promotion—inserted myself into the lineup.

That was when I was feeling ambitious. Mostly, I got stoned and watched movies at the second-run theater in Davis Square, rom-coms and costume dramas, gorgeous bloodletting and dick jokes. I'd snicker at the sappy parts and coat my arteries in Milk Duds, then walk outside into the silence of who I was.

One night, I stopped by a local pub and stared at a woman with such volcanic longing that she summoned the bouncer to escort me out.

How wretched was my poetry, really?

Owed to Water

It is said the ocean forgets everything
forgets the lash of lightning and the stones
it grinds to sand and the planks it swallows
without joy or renunciation

OK?

I wasn't ready to write about what was actually happening in my life. So I ravaged *Roget's Thesaurus* and bound the resulting dreck into a manuscript titled, unpretentiously, *Seven Essential Dreams*. Today, the process would be much easier. I could just type: *Write me some emo poems, ChatGPT.* But back then I had to compose each of these suicide notes by hand. Afterward, I sat on my porch, in a postcoital pout, awaiting the soft weep of rain.

My dad suggested therapy. I hated him for it, then went to see a psychiatrist who reminded me, a little, of my mother (also a psychiatrist) and who informed me, after our first session, that she didn't have room for me in her schedule. I staggered onto the sidewalk and burst into tears. As if in a dream, or a bad poem, one of my students appeared. We both had to pretend it wasn't happening, that she would not now race back to campus to inform the rest of the class.

Around this time, my mother flew to Boston for a series of interviews that represented the final exam of her psychoanalytic training. She was a nervous wreck that week, preoccupied in a manner I recognized from childhood. At dinner one night, I mentioned that I'd been writing poetry. "I once dated a poet," my mother said distractedly. "A million years ago, at Antioch. Do you know Mark Strand?"

"Mark Strand," I said. "Oh my God! Are you serious? I just saw him read." And so on.

I had long since renounced the practice of showing her my pain. For years, I'd been playing the role of her charming youngest son, the one trying to be a writer across the country. But having her in town, right across the table, awakened an ancient desperation. I wanted her to comfort me. My brain has spared me a reliable memory of that meal. I remember that there were French fries involved and that I started to cry. Or maybe I held it together until later. Either way, she knew I was having some kind of breakdown.

"I'm sorry you're struggling, Stevie," she said. "But I've got a lot on my mind. This is a big week for me."

I hate telling you this. I hate that it happened. My mother was the person I loved most in the world. She was the person whose devotion to literature had become my own. She was also tired of caring for needy, self-absorbed men. The point isn't that she was a bad mom. The point is that we had no idea, in that particular moment, how to reach each other. We were lost in private orbits of doubt.

SHE DIED IN MARCH OF 2016, my mother, after an awful battle with cancer.

It was a rough time in our national history, as you'll recall. All over the country, crowds gathered in arenas to chant, led by an unloved boy who had grown into a sad, cruel man. The central feature of these events was the expression of sadism toward some perceived enemy. Their psychic purpose was to purge doubt, to bury it beneath roars of grievance. The TV footage was hypnotic, as if a Nuremberg rally had been reimagined as a flea market.

We live with mystery. But we don't like the feeling.

Demagogues and tyrants recognize this instinctively. They're not running against a party or a population. They're running against compassion.

The election allowed one segment of the country to inflict its pain on everyone else. This took the form of policies that abrogated the rights of the weak and enriched the powerful. But the assault included a more pervasive effort to frighten and confuse, to make us feel what the poet Wallace Stevens described as the "pressure of the real," an incessant drumming of bad news that suggests the world is too urgently fucked up to justify the work of artists.

Wallace argued that literature was the place where we could resist the pressure of the real and thereby preserve our capacity to imagine, to contemplate, to dream, to drift in a state of not knowing.

That all sounds quite romantic. But it's hard to ignore the fresh disgraces that lurk within our browsers and remotes and easy to see ourselves as blameless victims. This manner of thinking is inherently unfriendly to our creative work. We would do better as writers to abandon that sense of assurance, to accept the general condition of our hearts and minds (and our country) as one of disequilibrium.

DISEQUILIBRIUM IS A TOUGH SELL, as the writer Charles D'Ambrosio observes, in a culture "crowded with public figures who speak exclusively from positions of final authority, issuing an endless stream of conclusions." We tend to hide our uncertainty, as if it were something shameful "that we are more intimately bound to one another by our kindred doubts than our brave conclusions."

D'Ambrosio was addressing nonfiction, specifically journalism. But his words apply, even more profoundly I would argue, to fiction writers. And they go a long way toward explaining why my initial drafts (and maybe yours, too) are so confusing.

Here's what is usually happening when I begin a story. First, I haven't quite worked out what the story is about. I have, at most, a few stray associations, a fragment of dialogue, a snagged memory, the faint outlines of a plot. My central feeling is one of doubt. If the project in question is a novel, multiply by a factor of ten.

Alas, rather than confronting this doubt by stepping back and figuring out if there's an actual story amid my musings, I do something even sneakier: I inflict my doubt on the reader. It's my way of punishing them for expecting me to know what I'm doing, to have the whole thing figured out and ready to lay before them just so.

This is not my conscious experience, of course. Consciously, I'm just lunging about for the next sentence, the next plot point, the next splendid description. But even as I learn more about my characters, as their dreams and fears begin to coalesce, I often conceal this data from the reader—hello again, *informational equity*—because I experience this withholding as a form of authority. A reader mired in doubt is in no position to judge the merits of the story in question or its insecure author.

There are, of course, other reasons that I foist doubt upon the reader. I forget that the reader isn't me, doesn't have access to my memories, hasn't been along for the journey of discovery. I fear that being upfront will violate some literary code of subtlety. I'm wary of the pain I might encounter and, especially in my non-fiction work, concerned about exposing my private tribulations, or those of my beloveds. Whatever the reasons, the result is the same: I mire the reader in *my* confusion, rather than that of my characters.

I'm not the only one making this category error. As the fiction editor of a literary magazine, I rejected 90 percent of our submissions for the simple reason that they were needlessly confusing.

To be clear: the stories we tell (if they are honest) should be full of doubt. Because we, as a species, are full of doubt. In fact, our deepest stories *arise* from our bewilderment. They represent a productive engagement with that bewilderment—a creative struggle to understand and make meaning from our destructive impulses, our disappointments and delusions, our unresolved traumas, the vaults of mayhem we calmly drag around.

POETS ACCEPT DOUBT AS part of their process, which is probably, as I think about it, why I sought refuge in poetry. I wanted to write without the pressures of narrative construction bearing down on me. Unfortunately, I couldn't bring along an honest accounting of my doubt. Instead, like some overgrown adolescent, I used poetry as a license to indulge and obscure.

Only in the past decade have I begun to accept poems for what they are: deftly constructed spaces where writers invite strangers to share in their sense of wonder and mystification. There are all sorts of poems. Some describe landscapes and recount epic feats. Others resurrect childhood, confront human depravity, commemorate the passions of everyday life, the bursts of joy and injury exploding all around us.

The poems that most enchant me are about doubt. Elisa Gonzalez's "In Quarantine, I Reflect on the Death of Ophelia" is angry lamentation, delivered from the depths of our most recent plague: isolation, a feverish lover, the greed of capitalism on full display outside her window. Gonzalez writes:

> But if I am alone, and if I am lonely, and if I am not
> alone in loneliness, and if the everyone
> together suffers, and if this everyone suffers and dies by
> the unguided motion of matter, and if

also by the motion of craven, murderous men, and if also
by the motion of money, and if of course
you were always going to die, Ophelia, and if even so
your death remains unforgivable,
then what are the questions I should ask?

That's the whole point: to remain humble and curious before the fluctuations of your own consciousness, to ask questions, to resist dogma, to persist in doubt. *So get your cut-up heart away from / What you think you know.* That's how Dorothea Lasky puts it, in her rambunctious ode, "I Like Weird Ass Hippies." Stop pretending to have it all figured it out.

Your job, as Matthew Zapruder observes, is to try to stand "in an actual stance of mystery towards the world." This phrase comes from his poem, "Pocket," which begins as a sly examination of the mundane and culminates with a contemplation of a pocket's darkness, its unknowability:

Like the bottom of the sea. But without
the blind florescent creatures floating
in a circle around the black box which along
with tremendous thunder and huge shards
of metal from the airplane sank down and settled
here where it rests, cheerfully beeping.

In my reading of the poem, this metaphor represents the futility of believing that we will ever know the full story recorded on that black box. We have to accept that we are the "blind florescent creatures" who can illuminate the shape of our uncertainty, and even hear its cheerful beeping, but remain help-less in our wishes for a full revelation.

WHEN I REVISIT THESE POEMS, my mind flashes to a partic-ular moment in ninth grade, when my English teacher, a bril-liant ham by the name of Jim Farrell, read us the first chapter of *The Catcher in the Rye*. I was hypnotized by the voice of Holden Caulfield, at once sly and bereft, but mostly I loved how honest Holden was about his own confusion. He wasn't on some epic quest to process his nervous breakdown. He was simply having it, on the page, hurtling through his lost weekend in New York City, offending the phonies, worrying over the ducks in Central Park, sobbing before his little sister.

Later on, I would find the same quality in the short stories that led me to abandon journalism: Lorrie Moore's addled her-oines, Barry Hannah's discombobulated Southerners, the ecstatic fuckups who populated *Jesus' Son*. To write so openly about doubt struck me as a revolutionary act. I had spent years hiding my own, mistaking insecurity for weakness.

We're all the same way. We present to the world a version of ourselves brimming with assurance, free of anguish, in control. We know it's a lie, but we see everyone else participating in that lie; the result is a vast and insoluble loneliness. This is why read-ers yearn for the company of your doubt.

As writers, we have to allow our characters to stumble, to fail, to wander off the trail and into bewilderment. We have to stop regarding our own misspent years as personal failures. Yes, we were drinking too much, ruining friendships, hurling our bodies before our hearts. Yes, we were unable to get out of bed. Yes, we got fired, got dumped, got arrested, got hospitalized. Yes, we needed help. But we were also, in the midst of all that, deeply alive. Pathetic as we might have seemed from the outside, we were working our asses off to change, to grow, to forgive.

I see that now: all the work I was doing during my year of bad poetry. I was sad and isolated and creatively confused. But I wrote every day. I got my ass into therapy, which helped me recognize that poems were not my given path. I lacked the patience, the tolerance for ambiguity, the self-awareness. I needed the narrative ballast of stories.

Years later, I would convert some of my bad poems into extremely short stories, which they had been, all along. Others proved irredeemable. They were still quite instructive. I eventually self-published them in a book called *Bad Poetry*, with essays that allowed me to unpack precisely how each poem descended into vagary, illogic, bigotry. Hiding behind even the worst of them was a true story I wasn't ready to tell yet, usually a story about how confused I was, how ashamed, how lost.

We always turn away from unbearable feeling. We want to feel sure of ourselves. We want to skip the part of the story where the hero falls apart. It's an instinct. But that's the story the reader wants to hear, the one only another human being in pain can tell them.

FREE WRITE

Write about an era of disequilibrium in your life. It could be that summer after college, when you were adrift and out of control. Or a weekend upstate, when your poise ran out and you spiraled. It could be a period triggered by some discernible injury: a sudden death, a romantic disaster, a bad diagnosis. Or a time when you expected to feel exultant—such as the birth of a child—but were instead besieged by doubts. Resist the urge to figure it all out. Stick with how you behaved and what you felt, the rhythm and rituals of those mad days. What particular scenes or moments do you still remember? How did you survive them? Go back there. Tell us about it. Slow down where it hurts. Slow down where it gets confusing.

Fiction writers: same deal, only you can write about a character (who may or may not have certain memories in common with you).

HOW TO WRITE SEX
SCENES WITHOUT SHAME

M ost of us, whether we like it or not, have an erotic life. It's
a part of the human arrangement. Our sexual drive is primal, often overpowering. It causes us to think things we'd rather
not think, to behave in ways we know to be destructive, to harbor wants that will remain unrequited. It's a source of tremendous vitality, occasional transgression, and consistent imbalance.
For this reason, humans have devised various systems of thought
that seek to stigmatize and even criminalize our sexual impulses.
(I'm looking at you, organized religion.) These efforts are, let's
face it, a testament to the power of our libidinal urges.

Given all this—how much sex matters to us, how much joy
and risk it awakens, how much it reveals about us—the question
I wish to pose to my fellow writers is this: Why the hell aren't
you writing *more* sex scenes? Aren't you curious about such a
fundamental aspect of the people you're writing about? Can you
really know them entirely if you don't know their kinks?

Alas, writers are subject to the same hang-ups as the rest of
the population. We, too, have been told—by our parents, our

teachers, our pastors, and our government—that sex is dangerous, profane, and, above all, private. We know that our characters fantasize about sex and worry about sex and have sex, but all this thinking and feeling remains governed by a collective code of silence.

In publishing, this silencing used to be enforced through blue laws. These days, the means of suppression are subtler. If we dare to write about sex explicitly, our stories will be deemed "erotica" and relegated to the red-light district of literature. I say this as someone whose stories have regularly appeared in the *Best American Erotica* anthology. Frankly, I should wear that as a badge of honor. But the very fact that there *is* a *Best American Erotica*—as differentiated from *Best American Short Stories*—underscores my point: a story can be about sex, or it can be about the inner life, but it can't be about both.

I myself fall victim to this mindset. In my essay about building round characters, it did not occur to me, until just now, that I failed to pose the following questions: What is your protagonist's relationship to sex? What was she taught about sex, and by whom? What are the formative moments in her sexual history? How much does she think about sex? What sort of partners, if any, does she seek out? What sort of sex turns her on, or frightens her, or both? How much does sex represent pleasure? How much does it represent power? How much punishment?

I could go on and on here. Answering every single one of these questions would help us better understand our protagonists.

So let's just say it: the biggest problem when it comes to sex scenes is that *they never get written.* They never get written because of our own inhibitions and because, to one degree or another, we suffer from performance anxiety. This is why writers so often skip from the part where the lovers are fumbling out of their clothes to the part in the morning, where the lovers are sipping some symbolic fluid—bitter coffee or sweet pulpy orange juice—their rude parts (and their hearts) safely tucked away.

This pressure obtains even when we do muster the courage to write sex scenes, and it leads to all the mistakes associated with pressure: unnecessary similes and metaphors, needless obfuscation, genital euphemisms, histrionics that wind up feeling imposed by the author instead of experienced by the characters.

But what if we removed the pressure for our sex scenes to be sexy? What if we freed ourselves to write about sex as we actually experience it, which is, yes, sometimes sexy, but also: doubt-choked, distracted, guilt-ridden, angry, sorrowful.

This is why I write stories with graphic sexual content. Not because I'm a pervert, or wish to embarrass my relatives, but because I want to place my characters in emotionally dangerous situations. The point isn't to undress them, or gawk at their gyrations, but to explore what they're thinking and feeling in the midst of such a vulnerable activity.

It feels especially important to break the silence around sex because that silence has helped preserve, and even promote, a patriarchal and heteronormative power structure that essentially erases the erotic experience of women, gay people, trans people, old people—anyone who isn't a straight dude.

This includes the profound risks that such groups incur. For most of human history, gay and trans people have had to suppress their identities and sexual urges or risk their lives. Women were considered marital property. In the world of pornography, they still exist largely as carnal chattel, slaves to male domination and gratification.

And for all the lip service paid to gender equality, a stark asymmetry still prevails. Women who engage in sexual relations still run the risk of reputational harm, exploitation and abuse, pregnancy and the loss of bodily autonomy. We've put a few celebrity abusers in jail, but 74 million Americans, many of them women, voted for an avowed sexual predator in 2020.

There are literary voices who offer a more candid, inclusive, nuanced portrayal of sex—all hail Melissa Febos, Alan Hollinghurst, and Mary Gaitskill, among others—but it's still hard to imagine them being afforded the literary respect that John Updike and Philip Roth have long enjoyed. As Michael Cunningham observed, after publishing his novel, *The Hours*: "I can't help but notice that when I finally write a book in which there are no men sucking each other's dicks, I suddenly win the Pulitzer Prize."

The story "Cat Person" became a viral sensation a few years ago precisely because Kristen Roupenian dared to write an explicit scene that captured what practically every straight woman has experienced multiple times: sex that is technically consensual but deeply upsetting. The story chronicles the one-night stand of Margot, a twenty-year-old undergrad, and Robert, a man fourteen years her senior. They wind up back at his place, where the sweet nothings sour:

> Looking at him like that, so awkwardly bent, his belly thick and soft and covered with hair, Margot recoiled. But

the thought of what it would take to stop what she had set in motion was overwhelming; it would require an amount of tact and gentleness that she felt was impossible to summon. It wasn't that she was scared he would try to force her to do something against her will but that insisting that they stop now, after everything she'd done to push this forward, would make her seem spoiled and capricious, as if she'd ordered something at a restaurant and then, once the food arrived, had changed her mind and sent it back.

Margot's complicity isn't the product of intimidation, but expedience, and a certain capitulation to her vanity. She gets herself turned on by imagining his arousal and they stumble on to a consummation governed by the desolate, disembodied mechanics of pornography. Margot feels like "a doll made of rubber, flexible and resilient, a prop for the movie that was playing in his head," Roupenian writes. "At the end, when he was on top of her in missionary, he kept losing his erection, and every time he did he would say, aggressively, 'You make my dick so hard,' as though lying about it could make it true. At last, after a frantic rabbity burst, he shuddered, came, and collapsed on her like a falling tree, and crushed beneath him, she thought, brightly, This is the worst life decision I have ever made! And she marveled at herself for a while, at the mystery of this person who'd just done this bizarre, inexplicable thing."

How many millions of young women, and men, have typed some flirty words into their phones, downed a few drinks, and cast their bodies before their hearts, only to arrive at the same mystification? Roupenian refuses to reduce hook-up culture to a set of disposable experiences. Even when the participants mimic the glandular detachment of porn, sex remains profound and revealing.

As writers, we should be brave and curious enough to explore the many contexts of sexuality in the lives of our characters (hook-up sex, break-up sex, courtship sex, marital sex, IVF sex, pregnancy sex, postpartum sex, postmenopausal sex) as well as the emotional functions of sex (revenge sex, healing sex, rebellion sex, ego-boost sex, dutiful sex). We should consider what forms sexuality takes for people who are differently oriented, differently abled, victims of sexual abuse, the aged, the mentally ill, the morbidly obese, for those bound by religious or moral prohibitions. We should approach sexuality as a path to illumination. Which means that the most powerful sex scenes are those that lead characters toward revelations they might otherwise dodge.

I'm thinking here about a piece of advice that Elizabeth Gilbert passed along to me years ago. Actually, the advice came from a romance novelist Gilbert consulted as she was writing *The Signature of All Things*. Gilbert was struggling to figure out how to write about the sexual life of Alma Whittaker, the novel's heroine.

The romance novelist urged Gilbert to think about the character in question and to simply imagine—given her temperament and circumstances—how she would have sex. Gilbert knew that Alma had a strong sexual drive, but also that this drive would have been difficult to express in the nineteenth century, particularly for a woman of her social standing and intellectual aims. And so Gilbert—bless her—granted Alma an outlet. Throughout the book, she retreats to the privacy of a small closet where certain thoughts make "wild demands upon her body." She lifts her skirts, opens her legs, and begins "frantically exploring her spongy petals, trying to find the devil who hid in there, eager to erase that devil with her hand." It, uh, works:

> She felt an unraveling. The hurt in her quim turned to something else—an up-fire, a vortex of pleasure, a chimney-effect of heat. She followed the pleasure where it led. She had no weight, no name, no thoughts, no history. Then came a burst of phosphorescence, as though a firework had discharged behind her eyes, and it was over. For the first conscious moment of her life, her mind was free from wonder, free from worry, free from work or puzzlement. Then, from the middle of that marvelous furred stillness, a thought took shape, took hold, took over:
> *I shall have to do this again.*

Please note how faithfully Gilbert followed the counsel she was given. Alma desperately needs to experience erotic pleasure, to quiet her busy mind, to *relax*. She wishes to explore that part of herself. But she has no conventional romantic outlet. It's important to recognize the great variety of our sexuality expression, which resides in our fantasies and our solo explorations, as well as our congress with other bodies.

It's important, also, to acknowledge that we're often terribly ambivalent when it comes to experiencing sexual delight. Alma Whittaker returns to this closet time and again. But she never shakes loose from the shame of these episodes.

At the other end of the spectrum is Smilla Jaspersen, the heroine of Peter Høeg's Danish novel *Smilla's Sense of Snow*. Smilla is a biracial woman who operates with a fierce defiance and mistrust of the authorities, an attitude reflected in the nature of her coupling with her lover, Peter. "He has a light, fumbling brutality, which several times makes me think that this time it'll cost me my sanity," Smilla tells us. "In our dawning, mutual intimacy, I induce him to open the little slit in the head of his penis so I can put my clitoris inside and fuck him."

Well then.

This is why I urge my students to write sex scenes—because they inevitably reveal secret aspects of your characters. Not just their peccadillos, but motives that remain hidden from public view. In *Sula*, Toni Morrison's restless heroine returns to her hometown. While others scorn the destructive power of her promiscuity, Sula herself uses sex to express the grief she bears for accidentally killing a younger child years earlier. "It was the only place where she could find what she was looking for," Morrison writes. "Misery and the ability to feel deep sorrow." Her one steady lover, Ajax, likes for Sula to mount him "so he could see her towering above him and call soft obscenities up into her face." What others might see as the claiming of power is inextricably linked to punishment.

Consider this passage, from the novel *Spending*, by Mary Gordon, in which a divorced woman takes a new lover for the first time in many months.

He put his head between my legs, nuzzling at first. His beard was a little rough on the insides of my thighs. Then with his lips, then his tongue, he struck fire. I had to cry out in astonishment, in gratitude at being touched in that right place. Somehow, it always makes me grateful when a man finds the right place, maybe because when I was young so many of them kept finding the wrong place, or a series of wrong places, or no place at all. That strange feeling: gratitude and hunger. My hunger was being teased. It also felt like a punishment. I kept thinking of the word "thrum," a cross between a throb and a hum. I saw a flame trying to catch; I heard it, there was something I was after, something I was trying to achieve, and there was always the danger that I'd miss it, I wouldn't find it, or get hold of it. The terrible moment when you're afraid you won't, you'll lose it, it won't work, you won't work, it is unworkable and you are very, very desperate. At the same time, you want to stay in this place of desperation ... at the same time, you're saying to yourself, you're almost there, you're almost there, you can't possibly lose it now, keep on, keep on a bit longer, you are nearly there, I know it, don't give up, you cannot lose it. Then suddenly you're there.

How much of this passage is devoted to the physical act? Three brief, declarative sentences. So let's dispense with Foolish Creed Number One of writing sex scenes: *Thou shalt be explicit and name all the parts and note where they are going, and how the lubrication is progressing and so forth.* Nonsense.

The central event during any sexual interaction is thought. That's what Gordon conveys here: the ticker tape of cogitation that runs parallel to the happy hum of our bliss centers. She uses those great underutilized tools of the trade, syntax and sentence shape, to convey the upheaval within her heroine, how anxiety keeps breaking the rhythm of her ascent toward climax. This is primarily what we're witnessing: the heroine's struggle to allow herself pleasure, the anxiety that "it won't work" and therefore she won't work. Consider the words associated with sex: punishment, danger, hunger, afraid, terrible, desperate. As with Alma, the goal isn't just physical ecstasy, but the annihilation of thought.

I'm not suggesting that every story you write should include sex scenes. In fact, if you don't feel comfortable writing about sex, please don't.

By this, I mean writing about sex as an emotional experience, not a form of titillation. Sex scenes are compelling only to the extent that they convey how vulnerable we all are when it comes time to get naked, how eager and frightened and ashamed and hopeful. You mustn't abandon your characters in their time of need. You mustn't make of them naked playthings with rubbery parts. You must love them, wholly and without shame, as they go about their human business.

FREE WRITE

'm going to ask you to do something that will sound counterintuitive, given the passages shared earlier: please write the worst sex scene you can. For inspiration, consider this snippet from a story entitled "A Seminal Release," which I selected as the judge of a bad erotica contest years ago:

> Jordan winked at the security guard and began darting her healthy pink tongue in and out of his right ear, and his dong began to well up with the juice of man. He undid her designer belt and slid his worker hands down her pants and into the folds of her thong underwear.

The scene you write need not be as heteronormative as this one, but it should be just as raunchy and overwritten. I'm ordering you to write smut because otherwise you'll get self-conscious, or filibuster, or both. It's a way of overruling your inhibitions and short-circuiting your performance anxiety. Go for at least twenty minutes. If you find yourself blushing or giggling, you're doing it right. When you're done, you can take a little time to forgive yourself and, if need be, take a shower. Then report back here. I mean it: go write. Now.

I'M GOING TO ASSUME that you've finished your sex scene. In looking over the scene, you may be amazed to find that—beneath all the problematic prose—something more tender is happening. The people you're writing about are expressing their desires, making them manifest in the world. Notice the ways in which hope is alive here, and how power is operating. Notice how certain hidden parts of each character have become visible. Notice any sensual details. Notice that something emotional happened that you weren't expecting.

If you've got the stamina, try a revision. Strike through the vile language and cartoonish kinks. Consider the glory of what remains.

PART III

MEDITATIONS

WRITER'S BLOCK: A LOVE STORY

HOW TO WRITE EGOLESS PROSE, AT LEAST FOR A LITTLE WHILE

The moment you sit down to write, two forces bear down on you. The first is an absolute conviction in the importance of your work, the shivery sense that you have been called to the language in some spiritual capacity, that you (and you alone) have stories the world must hear, that these stories are ready to spill out of you with the hot urgency of scripture and that when they do you will be recognized as a rare talent, a writer of the first order and eventually—why fight it?—the Messiah.

You are not the Messiah.

But this mindset is generative in nature. It tends to produce a lot of work, even if this same work later makes you cringe.

The second force is the creeping suspicion that any sustained effort to write is doomed, that you will never transcribe the story so perfectly arranged in your mind, will never convey the insight and depth of emotion sloshing around in there, and that the best result you can hope for is that your mother will drive to your apartment with a Crock-Pot full of soup and ask why you're depressed.

Bad news: you will never rid yourselves of these opposing forces.

Good news: your job is not to make them go away, but to mitigate, and tolerate, the fluctuation between them.

It will help to take a step back from the keyboard and consider the essential nature of the activity. What is writing, if you boil away all the romance? Writing is decision-making. Nothing more and nothing less. What word? Where to place the comma? How to shape the paragraph? Which characters to undress and in what manner? It's relentless.

If you refuse to pass judgment on these decisions, if you walk around thinking you're the Messiah, you'll wind up settling for inferior decisions, by which I mean imprecise, contrived, solipsistic ones. If, on the other hand, you condemn your decisions, you'll lose the improvisatory momentum upon which all narrative construction depends.

The only surefire solution is to develop the capacity to access your decisions without second-guessing your talent. I believe the most effective way to expand this capacity is to appraise the work of other writers, whose decisions you can see more clearly than your own. The goal is to attain that elusive state in which your decision-making becomes intuitive rather than labored.

This sounds lovely. But often in the midst of a writing project, in the midst of the life surrounding that writing project, the second force takes over, and we are overrun with feelings of dread, helplessness, and self-loathing. The technical term is *Writer's Block*.

Amid the skittish egos of the literary world, Writer's Block has assumed a status akin to the Black Plague, an affliction that forces us into quarantine. We just sort of melt from view for a while, off-loading the worst of ourselves onto paid help and loyal beloveds.

I want to dispel some of the myths about Writer's Block, and undo the mysteries that surround the condition. What's happening when we feel blocked? What can we do to find our way back to the keyboard? Can we accept Writer's Block as a potential ally to our creativity?

The first thing that needs to be said is that writers get blocked almost constantly. During the composition of this very paragraph, I stopped typing thirty-seven times (I counted), stumped as to what I wanted to say next, and how. I got up and made a snack. I went outside to chase away the woodchuck living beneath our storage shed. I came back inside and turned off the app that turns off my internet and spent a solid half hour researching how to poison a woodchuck. I considered what would happen if I poisoned the woodchuck—or worse yet, the *baby woodchuck*—and my wife found out. I made a bunch of linguistic tweaks, most of which I unmade, before erasing the whole paragraph and starting over. At every phase of this extremely shitty and inefficient process, I was suffering a block, a moment in which doubt and indecision overtook my faith. I am still eyeing this paragraph suspiciously.

So let's please stop treating Writer's Block as a binary: either we're flowing or we're blocked. It's more precise to say that Writer's Block is the extreme end of a spectrum, where the inhibitive impulses that almost always accompany our decisions become debilitating. We feel a futility so potent that we stop making decisions altogether.

Crazily enough, Writer's Block is sometimes a symptom of progress. I have a lot of students who travel the same arc I did in grad school. They put in long hours critiquing the work of their comrades. This sharpens their critical faculty. When they return to their own prose, they are suddenly confronted by flaws that had been invisible. It's brutal.

But what's really happening? They're holding themselves to a higher standard, taking their task more seriously. It can feel like being cast out of Eden. The writer has to leave the paradise of innocence (making decisions free of judgment) and face the true nature of her work, the psychological and emotional challenges of literary art. Welcome to the big show.

I'VE BEEN STALLED CREATIVELY so many times over the years that it can be hard for me to distinguish between periods of genuine Writer's Block and eras in which I've managed to avoid deep creative work by focusing on other pursuits, such as making money or promoting a book or poisoning baby woodchucks. But I certainly remember the worst of my blocks.

Back in 2003, for instance, I fell into a sustained depression. As is often the case, the trigger was a major creative disappointment. Two years earlier, I'd published my first book, a collection of short stories. I naturally expected this triumph would banish all the doubt I had ever felt, vanquish my rivals, and compel old girlfriends to drunk-dial me in the middle of the night. People would probably also throw money at me as I walked down the sidewalk. Instead, the book sold a few hundred copies and my agent told me to write a novel.

I wrote every day, convinced the book would be a smashing success. My fingers were typing. My characters were gallivanting. From the outside, it looked like I was working. Hell, I *was* working. After two years, I had 850 pages, which I sent off to my agent. Several months passed. There is no need to catalogue the multitude of panicky, passive-aggressive emails I composed during this span, though for poetic effect, I would estimate the count at 850 million.

Then came a brief conversation. Less than a minute. My agent had read what she could of the manuscript and felt it would be better for us to part ways. She was right, of course, which didn't stop me from loathing her.

Soon enough, the hatred burned off and I fell right through the floor. There was no point in writing. About the only thing that got me out of bed during those months was the desire for chocolate. Back then, I was eating in such volume, and on such a meager budget, that I took to buying direct from the Haviland Chocolate factory, just a short drive from my apartment in Somerville. There was a little shop on the first floor that sold seconds, meaning chocolates that were, like me, defective in some way. Often the defect was an excess of chocolate coating, or the accidental bonding of two pieces into one. I could purchase a two-pound box of mint patties for three dollars and a bulging bag of conjoined Clark bars for a buck fifty.

I spent a lot of time in that shop, inhaling chocolate fumes and pondering the miracle of industrial candy production. At a certain point, rent became a pressing concern. A solution soon presented itself. As an apostate journalist, I pitched the local alt weekly a story about Haviland Chocolate. The moment I set foot in the factory, my sadness dissolved. The elevators smelled like Halloween. Massive copper cauldrons of caramel bubbled. Conveyer belts carried marshmallow bunnies through curtains of shimmering chocolate. I had found a world that awakened my attention and curiosity, that brought me alive again.

I decided I would write a book about candy. I didn't write a book proposal, I just started flying all over the country and bullshitting my way into the little factories where they made weird regional candy bars like the Idaho Spud and the Twin Bing.

When the book was done, I sent it out to a bunch of agents, all of whom agreed it would never sell. It was too strange. One said he didn't know where it would be shelved in Borders, which is a lot funnier now than it was at the time. The book *was* genuinely odd: part ode to candy, part angsty confession, part travelogue.

I stuffed the draft in a drawer. I dug it out again only because my writer friends kept asking to read it. Their enthusiasm gave me confidence to send it out to a few editors, one of whom bit. But even after *Candyfreak* was published, I regarded it as a lark. I had failed at the novel and settled for pop-culture journalism.

I now view the situation more generously: I wrote my way out of a sustained block. This block, in fact, had helped me cast off a certain writerly vanity that was holding me back. Rather than asking, *What sort of book* should *I be writing?* I was able to ask a much more useful question: *What sort of book do I* want *to write?*

A simpler way of putting it would be this: I lowered the bar.

When people ask me how to deal with Writer's Block, that's my essential advice: *lower the bar*. Blocks result from putting too much pressure on ourselves. Set aside (for now anyway) the big project intended to validate your ego. Focus on what will get you to the keyboard, what feels attainable. Write for twenty minutes. Or ten.

And make sure you have friends around, for support and for the reality check.

WHAT I'M SUGGESTING HERE isn't a regimen of bonbon consumption and self-adulation, but something more like a temporary reprieve from the hardship of judgment. Because judgment leads to insecurity. And *all bad decisions at the keyboard arise from insecurity*, from little moments of doubt in which our attention shifts from the drama of the story in question to the yammering of ego need.

As this happens, we stop asking the questions that drive our stories forward: Who am I writing about? What do they desire? What endangers them? Can they be saved? We start asking smaller, self-involved questions. Will this metaphor impress the reader? Am I smart enough to pull this off? Funny enough? Deep enough?

We start to perform rather than engage in storytelling. We leap into scene without context. We overwrite. We orchestrate coincidences and calamities to goose the action.

When my students talk about these decisions in workshop, they use language that betrays their insecurity. They talk about how readers will get bored if they reveal too much too soon, as if plot elements should be scattered about like breadcrumbs, to lure the wayward along. They fear readers will deem them histrionic if they dramatize moments of conflict. Or dull if they don't prettify the language. These decisions, which are intended to entice and placate the reader, have the opposite effect. The reader winds up confused and thwarted. The writer, encountering this, winds up feeling, well, blocked.

It's a negative feedback loop.

So how do we disrupt the loop?

Previously, I recommended lowering expectations and shifting to a less fraught project. But I know from personal experience that it's possible to confront Writer's Block more directly.

The first step is to take a deep breath and recognize that the manuscript's flaws are not an indictment of your talent or your right to tell the story. They are merely a set of imperfect decisions you made at a particular moment.

It's important to consider precisely *how* these decisions were imperfect, without succumbing to the opera of self-doubt. You have to be able to study your decisions with detachment, to fig-ure out why you made them in the first place.

If you're anything like me (bad news: you are), you wanted your writing to address certain primal yearnings. Namely, to be seen, heard, acknowledged, understood, admired, and—hell, let's just get to the basement of this thing—loved. And you know what? You deserve all of that. Try to resist the urge to patholo-gize these needs or to cast them as weakness. They're an essential part of your engine to create.

It's only when these yearnings overpower your creative inten-tions that they undermine your work. Rather than becoming immersed in the world of the characters and their struggles, the reader continually encounters the writer, who stands in the way of the story, frantically mugging, hoping you will admire his fine manners of thought and feeling.

Your sentences start to betray the doubt you feel about your-self instead of exploring the bewilderments that haunt your characters: how to survive the sorrows of childhood, say, why we choose the wrong lovers. These are the mysteries your readers are struggling to understand. They are turning to you not for answers but solace, the promise that they are not alone in these struggles. If you can dial your ego down, an entire imaginative space opens up, into which the muse can willingly enter.

What happens in moments of peak creativity should be con-sidered a dividend of sublimation. It's not that we make our feelings go away; we're able to transmit them to our characters. We summon the courage to lay them bare and the grace to grant them a forgiveness we rarely attain ourselves.

When my writing is going well, I fall into a flow state marked by intense focus, imaginative rigor, freedom of association, and psychic momentum. Simply put: the story becomes more interesting to me then how well I'm telling it. The ego drama of Am I Good Enough gives way to the larger and more generous drama of whether the heroine will find love, or ruin, and will come to know the truth of herself in the process.

Egoless prose.

That's the term a colleague used recently. She was describing the rapture induced when she sensed that 100 percent of the writer's skill and attention was devoted to her characters.

But you can be sure the author in question suffered through periods of Writer's Block along the way. She may be suffering through a block right now, as you read this. This should not be taken as bad news. It just means that all creative states are temporary. Just because you're blocked today doesn't mean you'll be blocked tomorrow.

Faith is the capacity to hold on to hope amid despair.

ONE MORE STORY FROM THE VAULT. This one takes place just a few years ago. I'm three-quarters of the way through a novel that feels like the best thing I've written in years. I've sent the first hundred pages off to the editor I trust most in the world, and he's just returned with good news and bad news. He thinks it stands a chance. But it needs major revisions.

Ever since I received his note, I've been waking at 4 a.m., churning with dread. My wife lies next to me, drowsily assessing the situation. She knows what happens next, that I'll tromp downstairs to my office and stare at the screen for hours, that the hole I'm digging for myself will get deeper. There's not a lot she can say. She's a writer, too. I snap at my kids. My therapist recommends an antidepressant. What if I'm not cut out to write a novel, he asks. Would that be so terrible?

Back in my basement, amid the candy wrappers and woodchuck poison, I rewrite the opening of the book. Four times. I'm making decisions, but I don't believe in them. This goes on for months. Then I do something totally out of character: I surrender to the possibility my asshole therapist is right—that I'll never write a novel.

No trumpets blare. I'm just tired of defining myself by what I can't do, by some ancient and frankly vain notion of what I'm meant to achieve.

Within a few weeks, I start poking at a story about a young girl growing up in the California of my youth. She's smart and brave and desperate with yearnings that lure her into danger. Pretty soon the police are involved, then the FBI. It's not a novel yet, just a story that keeps expanding. Every day, I arrive at the keyboard and my heroine is still there, taking risks, pushing her luck. I'm so in love with her, so worried about her. For the first time in years, I'm writing egoless prose.

I know the block will be back, if it ever even left. There's nothing shameful in any of this. We all go through it. We're all afraid we will never be worthy of love. The fear takes us under for a while. It feels like drowning. But we're not drowning. We get to breathe.

ADVENTURES IN WORKSHOP LAND

IN SEARCH OF A HEALING COMMUNITY

L et's start with a statement likely to rankle: people who take writing workshops are going in search of themselves. This is not their entire motive; it's certainly not their conscious one. Aspiring writers don't think to themselves: *I really want to understand myself better. Oh, I know: I'll sign up for a writing workshop!* They are thinking something more like: *This story is important to me, and I need some help figuring out how best to tell it.*

The goal of a writing workshop is not to therapize the participants, but to help them better tell a story that reveals themselves, in ways they might not even feel comfortable sharing with friends and family. This is obvious in memoir or personal essay. It's also true of fiction and poetry, works of imagination invariably guided (as we've seen) by the writer's obsessions, inner conflicts, unresolved emotions.

Everyone arrives in a state of extreme vulnerability—that's my point. Their work will be judged by a group of relative

STEVE ALMOND

strangers, whose job it is to offer suggestions for how the piece can be made deeper, more truthful. Whatever portion of them is on the page (experiences, anxieties, delusions) will suffer the same scrutiny. We can try to pretend the process is professional, technical, empirical. It's mostly personal.

For this reason, workshop leaders aren't just in the business of handing out sage advice. Their first and final task is to create a safe space for all the participants. This, too, sounds queasily therapeutic. It's not. The worst outcomes in any writing workshop arise from the participants not feeling safe.

An extreme example from my own time in the MFA salt mines: I was part of a small incoming class of fiction writers. The second-year cohort consisted of seven students, all of them men, all but one white. They were a loud, contentious, intimidating bunch. The workshop was optional for them, but they all enrolled because the teacher was the program's rising star, a relatively young guy whose story collection had just been reviewed, miraculously it seemed to us, by the *New York Times Book Review*. The second years were hungry for his feedback and his mentorship.

We first years walked into that classroom deeply intimidated, a feeling magnified by the camaraderie between this teacher and these second-year students, who would often head to a bar after class. The vibe of the workshop itself was often antagonistic. The goal, as I perceived it, was to register a criticism sharp enough to make the teacher take note. The incentive system was predicated on impressing the leader, not nurturing the writer.

148

I had come to the program after seven years in journalism and was myself an entitled white dude. I held my own in class. But the other first-year students were less vocal. One woman had spent most of her life struggling financially and still worked a full-time job, because the program hadn't given her any funding. She also had a disability that compromised her hearing. I liked her a lot. She struck me as someone who had endured more than the rest of us yet resisted becoming cynical.

One day she called me out of the blue and told me that our teacher had refused to workshop the story she submitted. It wasn't worthy of the group's consideration, he said. I can't remember the exact sequence of events—whether she called me before or after class. I have a vague recollection of glancing at her during the workshop in question, and seeing that her face was flushed. I remember, quite distinctly, that this woman, whom my mother would have described as a "tough cookie," began to cry on the phone. She left the program a few months later.

All teachers are entitled to their own process. There is no one "right" way to run a workshop. Some students thrive on this kind of creative Darwinism. But any style of pedagogy that stresses competition over collaboration can never feel entirely safe for any of the participants, because even the "winners"—the ones who earn protégé status and go on to get published—have adopted a doomed value system. They will eventually measure themselves against other writers and feel like losers. Personal achievement without generosity of spirit is a dead end.

The worst damage a workshop can do is to undermine a writer's aspirations, to sow doubts that lead them to question their worth, to humiliate their creative impulses into silence.

This is especially galling because the writers who arrive in a workshop the most vulnerable are the ones whose stories risk going untold. Because our society remains patriarchal and capitalistic and white supremacist and heteronormative and ableist, people like me (male, white, straight, etc.) enjoy an ingrained sense that we have a right to tell our stories. It's much harder for someone like my classmate to believe she enjoys the same right.

The goal of a workshop should be to infuse students with enthusiasm and humility and curiosity and faith, to make them eager to get back to the keyboard, so they can find ways to solve the problems the workshop has articulated.

This does not happen simply by offering praise and platitudes. There are, occasionally, students who arrive in class eager for applause and little more. But most students walk into a workshop knowing they need help. They want to be taken seriously as writers. The question then becomes: How can a workshop deliver precise and exacting advice while remaining an emotionally safe space? The answer is that radical candor requires radical empathy.

WHAT I'M ARGUING HERE is that a workshop can be completely honest about the work only if everyone trusts everyone else.

Every member is responsible for building this trust. But the workshop leader holds inordinate power. She makes the rules and sets the tone. From the moment she walks into the room, students are watching her to see how she conducts herself—not just what she says, but how and to whom, where she sits, with whom she makes eye contact.

In other educational settings, students seek proficiency. In a writing workshop, the leader often represents the fulfillment of a dream.

The first workshop leader I ever had was the novelist John DuFresne, who ran a community group for fiction writers on Friday afternoons, on the campus of the school where he taught, Florida International University. John was an established novelist with a full slate of classes and a family. The fact that he ran a free workshop for doofuses like me was an act of unthinkable generosity. His leadership style was kind, relaxed, egalitarian. This is partly why I found the vibe of my MFA workshops so alienating.

But (and this is a big but): I was bringing my own psychological baggage into those MFA workshops. I had been raised in a family of fractious boys. As I saw it, my parents had failed to curb our aggression. Thus, when our workshops turned cutthroat, I felt betrayed by my workshop leaders in a way that was—again, that word—*personal*. And I broadcast these feelings. I shook my head in frustration. I called one teacher out for bad-mouthing another writer. I wrote a foolishly candid letter for another professor's tenure file.

The net result is that I was banned from taking the workshop my second year. Both my workshop leaders refused to read my thesis. Neither would speak to me.

I doubt most MFA students experience this kind of rancor. I'm certainly sorry I did, and I've spent many years working to understand my contribution to this particular shit show. On the other hand, I learned a powerful lesson: as a workshop leader, you are always going to have intense, provocative students. *Never make it personal.*

A few years after I graduated, I was recruited to teach an MFA fiction class as a last-minute replacement. I was painfully earnest, underqualified, and nervous. My predominant memory of that workshop is my failure to intercede when a socially powerful student's feedback curdled into contempt. I told myself that I was showing restraint, refusing to "make it personal." But I can see now that I was abdicating my duties as a workshop leader. For whatever reasons—reasons that were really none of my business—he came into that class eager to foment dissent. I should have met with him and set a boundary.

Over the years, I've come to accept that people walk into a writing workshop with all sorts of hopes and hang-ups. Regardless of how you behave, the workshop leader is going to become a transference figure for certain students. My job is to direct our attention away from the drama in the room and toward the drama in the work we're there to discuss.

THE IMPLICIT QUESTION in all this is *how.*

My process begins before we meet as a class. I send a letter to students explaining my expectations for the class. (I want to highlight the word *expectations* because it's the same word that the novelist Matthew Salesses uses in his book *Craft in the Real World*, which I'll return to a bit later.)

Here are my expectations:

I ask that students read each submission, twice if possible, once for flow and a second time to mark up, noting passages they particularly enjoyed, along with any spots where they felt confused, or where the story bogged down or felt rushed. I'm not asking for a set of judgments so much as a *respectful* record of their line-by-line reactions to the piece.

This practice is integral to the workshop process in four distinct ways. First, this full set of marked-up manuscripts offers the writer a kind of granular audit of the piece. If eleven out of twelve readers found a particular passage affecting, they know that passage is working. If the same readers flagged another spot as disorienting, the writer knows it needs work.

Second, marking up manuscripts compels students to read actively, thinking about *why* particular decisions on the page elicit admiration or concern. As I've explained elsewhere, I believe writers learn more from critiquing the work of their colleagues than any other part of workshop, because they are able to identify achievements and missteps they are often blind to in their own work.

Third, having marked up the manuscript, the students have a road map for the letter of critique I ask them to write.

Fourth, and most important, the students are making an unspoken compact in fulfilling this expectation. The attention they devote to one another's manuscripts creates a sense of mutual obligation.

As the workshop leader, it's my job to model this generosity. My letters of critique are often four or five single-spaced pages.

They offer detailed praise and address craft issues such as narration, plot, and character that apply not just to the piece in question, but to the other manuscripts we'll be reading.

It's crucial that I devote this much attention to each piece because it's my job to lead the discussion, to make sure we're learning as much as possible from every manuscript. This is another point I emphasize before we meet. Students may be focused on the fate of the piece they bring to class, but the broader mission is to help students develop their own critical faculties.

Students can immediately sense when an instructor is mailing it in. I certainly could. I can still remember the day one of my favorite writers visited our MFA program to lead a workshop. He barely discussed the pieces under consideration. Instead, he delivered a set of boilerplate remarks. In my own teaching, I have, at times, fallen prey to distraction, or poor planning, and failed to read a piece as carefully as I should have. It always shows up in class, and it erodes trust.

If I'm asking my students to go deep, they have to know I'm doing the same thing.

THE SECOND ASK in my pre-class letter is that the students compose a single sentence summarizing what they take the piece to be about. This sounds incredibly reductive. But what all writers need, more than praise even, is the assurance that their comrades in workshop have made a good faith effort to apprehend their intentions.

I don't dictate how these sentences should be written. Some are broad and aphoristic. Others focus on the events of the story. Mine are long, reeling affairs, studded with semicolons, in which I try to identify the thematic concerns, the arc of the plot, the underlying emotional struggles. There's no right or wrong approach. It's like the parable of the blind men and the elephant. Each reader touches different aspects of the piece, based on their sensibility.

What's undisputable is their cumulative effect on the writer. They are deeply *affirmed*. This is especially true because often readers identify ambitions the writer hadn't fully brought into their own consciousness. More than pride, I see in their reactions a deep sense of trust: *They get what I'm trying to do.* If they don't feel that trust, they won't be able to absorb fully what their comrades have to say. They will be locked in state of defensive reactivity rather than optimistic reflection.

Over the course of a workshop, students come to embrace this exercise. Even those who initially regarded it as condescending come to see these summaries as an opportunity to offer their own reckoning with the piece. As they learn to home in on the writer's intentions, their sentences become more compassionate and insightful. They capture the quality of profound attention that is the underlying goal of every workshop.

TOO OFTEN, AS IN GRAD SCHOOL, I've been in workshops where the emphasis was criticism. There's a kind of grim predictability to this process. Each speaker offers a cursory compliment before opening fire. Not only does this overwhelm the person being workshopped, but it almost guarantees that the group's competitive anxieties will overrun its generous, communal impulses. Because what do you think is going to happen when the tables are turned?

More fundamentally, this approach defines the piece as something broken, in need of repair, rather than what it actually is: An artistic accomplishment that has yet to meet its full potential. This is why I ask students—after we've all read our one-sentence summaries—to share their favorite passages from the piece. I don't mean mentioning them (i.e., "I liked the part where Sheila confronts her ex-husband"). I mean directing the class to the passage in question ("second and third full paragraphs on page seven") and reading the words out loud, then speaking about how and why that passage excited them. I devote at least a third of our class time to this phase.

This is not merely to flatter the writer. It is an effort to reframe the goal of a workshop, which should be to celebrate the strongest moments in each story and help the writer bring the rest of the piece up to that level. That sounds simple enough. But the human brain fixates on criticism. The moment we hear disapproval, we can no longer retain praise.

By isolating and reading each moment of power, authenticity, and beauty, the entire class taps into that potential. Everyone starts believing. And not just in the piece being critiqued. Writers adopt a more hopeful attitude toward their own work.

A workshop cannot perform the arduous task of revision. But the best of them leave participants feeling energized and eager to revise. Attention is the crucial ingredient, but belief is essential, too.

THE LAST PHASE OF THE WORKSHOP is reserved for constructive criticism, which really just means: Don't be an asshole. Don't think you'll be rewarded for finding fault.

I urge students to ask questions but not hide behind vagaries. They should direct the class to the exact passage where they have concerns, and be concrete about the nature of those concerns. If they feel unmoored or strong-armed, can they point to the place on the page where that feeling begins? If language is an instrument of truth, where, exactly, does it feel false, or imprecise, or vague?

My role in all this is to direct the class to those spots where they fall out of the story, and to help us understand, as a group, how and why that's happening. Because I've read thousands of drafts as a teacher and editor, I tend to see patterns. Often reader confusion results from the absence of a strong narrator, for instance. If the writer hasn't figured out how to manage chronology, the reader feels jerked around. Writers often struggle to synthesize all the plot elements they've introduced.

In my view of storytelling, the most fundamental question for readers is who we're being asked to care about, what they desire, and what sort of trouble they encounter in pursuit of that desire. In other words, what promises is the piece making? Has our protagonist been forced to reckon with external obstacles and internal conflicts?

I'm speaking again of expectations, and in so doing I want to invoke a crucial point that Matthew Salesses raises. Namely, that every participant in a workshop comes into the room with their own experiences and sensibility, which determine their expectations. As a reader, and writer, I have a strong bias toward stories that push the characters, especially the protagonist, into emotional and psychological danger.

I grew up absorbing this particularly Western view of storytelling, and it's probably relevant that I'm also the child of two psychoanalysts. I'm pushing a set of expectations that may not line up with those of students from different backgrounds.

My central job as a workshop leader isn't to silence my expectations, but to accept that my experience as a writer doesn't make me the final authority. I have a particular set of dogmas, about narration, character development, scene construction, and so on. So long as these dogmas help my students tell the stories *they* feel called to tell, they are useful. But it's important for a workshop leader to acknowledge that his or her or their particular approach isn't the only way, or even the best way. I urge all my students to take what they can from our discussion, and to leave the rest aside.

HAVING SAID THIS, I want to emphasize that one of the most lamentable outcomes of any workshop discussion is the disorienting feeling that the writer's head is suddenly filled with a cacophony of voices, each making earnest recommendations, many of them contradictory. I sometimes think of this as the Focus Group Effect.

My role is to integrate what participants are saying, so the cacophony becomes something more like a chorus. That requires that I identify what I see as the major challenges in any piece and keep the class focused on them. If I sense the discussion is drifting into the weeds—by which I mean focusing on technical concerns, or a clash of sensibilities—my job is to redirect us to the piece's deepest ambitions.

Rather than settling for a catalogue of flaws, the question should be: What can the writer do to address these concerns? If the concern is pacing, can we point to passages where the writer would do well to streamline or slow down? If the concern is plausibility, can we help the writer develop character motivation earlier in the story?

My job as workshop leader isn't to dominate the discourse, but to direct the conversation, to amplify and expand on student comments, to draw connections between the work in question and other student manuscripts, and to point to published work that models how other writers have addressed the same concerns.

It's also my job to make sure that everyone feels empowered to offer their feedback, especially those who might be less comfortable speaking. Because I've been a part of workshops where the most assertive voices drown out others—I've been one of those assertive voices—I'll sometimes call on more deferential students. My goal isn't to put anyone on the spot, but to make sure every perspective in the room gets heard.

The collective aim here should be diagnostic, not prescriptive. I have zero tolerance for students who try to tell other students the story they should be writing, even when these ideas are offered in good faith. A workshop is not a brainstorming session. Our job isn't to describe the story we wish the writer in question had submitted, but to recognize, and help them realize, the story *they* came to tell.

SOME WORKSHOP LEADERS allow the writers being critiqued to speak throughout the workshop. My approach is to leave a few minutes at the end of class for the writer to ask questions, about the points made during the discussion, or specific issues the group didn't address. My reasoning here is that any manuscript submitted to an editor or agent has to speak for itself. It does not arrive with an author attached or a chance to dialogue. Hopefully, that will happen later, after the editor or agent in question has decided to take on the manuscript.

Salesses (and others) object to this "cone of silence" method, arguing that it casts the author into the background when they should be at the center of the discussion. As I see it, the subject of discussion in a workshop is the manuscript under consideration. That is: the decisions the author has made on the page, not their identity off the page.

I'm not suggesting that the author's identity doesn't matter. It would be naïve to pretend that writing workshops in America are bastions of diversity. They're not. Most participants have the wealth necessary to pay for and participate in a writing workshop. They are overwhelmingly white. (So is the publishing industry.) There is no doubt that writers from marginalized communities who submit to workshops are being judged by writers who are sometimes woefully ignorant of their lived experience.

If the discussion of these decisions descends into bigoted, or benighted assumptions, it is incumbent upon the workshop leader to address those directly. I once led a workshop in which a white student said, in reference to descriptions of the trauma suffered by enslaved characters, that the story had "great material." I asked the class to consider how it might feel to hear the suffering of your forebears described as "great material."

It is not the burden of an African American writer, or a gay writer, or an undocumented writer, or a blind writer, to serve as a representative of that lived experience. Readers who confuse the protagonist for the author, especially an author from a marginalized community, are assuming such writers have only one story to tell, which is both an insult to their imaginative and empathic capacities and a boundary around them.

At the same time, when writers from such communities *choose* to write about their lived experience, their comrades in a workshop have to be honest about their questions and confusions. The discussion is often one that redounds to the question of intended audience. I've thought about this a lot because I've led workshops for a decade at the Nieman Foundation, where half the students are foreign journalists. They often write pieces about their own country or region, in which they leave out a lot of historical context.

It's important for American readers, like me, to note the absence of this context. But it's equally important to acknowledge that such context may not be necessary, if the intended audience—a reader from the same region—already knows it. Not everyone is writing for the benefit of the dominant culture: Western, white, straight, male, etc.

When it comes to the question of audience, I urge my students to imagine a reader who is attentive, curious, and essentially ignorant of the world you're writing about. I do this because my agenda is for students to write pieces that are as inclusive and durable as possible, that can be understood and enjoyed by a reader who lives half a world away or a hundred years in the future. That's the long game.

THERE'S A LONG GAME when it comes to teaching a workshop, too. Obviously, I want students to depart inspired to rework their submissions. But most of all, I want them to improve their storytelling day by day. The best workshops inspire a collective commitment to learning. I stress affirmation and praise precisely because writers cannot summon the tools of learning—humility and curiosity—until they've turned down the dial on their ego needs.

Almost all students enter a workshop wondering if they will be the one among their peers to become a published author. Naturally, they look to the teacher for some indication. They approach me after class with some variation of the same question: "Do I have the talent to make it as a writer?"

There's no way for me to know. I have no idea what "making it as a writer" even means to the person asking the question. It could mean publishing a book to rave reviews from the *New York Times Book Review* or maintaining a daily writing practice or anything in between. This definition is likely to evolve over time.

I do know that talent is a lousy predictor of literary success. In thirty years, I've taught droves of supremely gifted writers, very few of whom made a career of writing. Others, who displayed no special affinity for the language, went on to publish bestsellers. The real question, with its unknowable answer, is this: Are you willing to do the lonely, dogged work? Are you capable of sustained learning? Can you find meaning in the process of writing, regardless of the outcome? Can you build the community you need to keep going?

I always urge my workshop students to reach out to the classmates who were good readers for them, to continue the practice of exchanging work, to hold one another accountable.

For years, I've listened to various pompous voices dispute whether creative writing can be taught. It's a fraudulent debate. Good teachers can and do help students demystify the elements of storytelling and understand how to make stronger decisions. Ask any published writer, or look in the back of their books, where they thank their various teachers.

No workshop leader can teach humility or determination. They *can* model those virtues.

THE MAN AT THE
TOP OF THE STAIRS

ON RENDERING THE INNER LIFE

O ver the past decade, my taste in literature—or at least my engagement with it—has shifted dramatically. I spend most my "reading time" reciting charming and insufferable tales to my children. *Curious George*, for instance, is both the account of an irascible chimp unleashed in the big city and the chilling tale of interspecies abduction. *Babar the Elephant* has the same ripe flavor of unacknowledged colonial predation, with the added twist that Babar clearly serves as a sexual slave to his rapacious octogenarian mistress. I could go on here but won't.

I mention these books not just because I know every goddamn word of them by heart, but because as I thought about how to discuss the "inner life" without sounding like a pretentious twit, my mind kept returning to one particular moment from the book *I'll Love You Forever* by Robert Munsch. It's about a mother who has a ritual of rocking her only child back and forth and singing him this song:

I'll love you forever,
I'll like you for always,
As long as I'm living
my baby you'll be.

As so often happens in children's books, things quickly get weird. The child grows into a teenager. The mother waits until he's asleep and picks him up and rocks him and sings to him. This ritual continues into his adulthood. The mom gets into her car and drives to his house and if the lights are out, she opens his bedroom window and crawls across the floor and, yes, she picks up this grown-ass man and rocks him and sings to him.

So OK. Potentially kinky, borderline criminal behavior. But also: sweet.

Eventually, the mom grows too old and sick to continue breaking into her son's home and rocking him to sleep. So the ritual is reversed. He drives to her house and picks up his mother and rocks her and sings to her.

Then comes the moment that haunts me. Munsch writes:

When the son came home that night, he stood for a long time at the top of the stairs.

AND THAT'S IT. That's the line. *When the son came home that night, he stood for a long time at the top of the stairs.*

I could tell you, of course, what the man does next, that he then goes into the room where his own new baby daughter is sleeping and that he picks her up and rocks her back and forth and sings to her. But that's not the part that sticks with me. Because that's not the part that reveals his inner life, all the sadness and bewilderment—the ecstatic paralysis—that grips him at the top of those stairs, as he seeks to reckon with the death of his mother.

A LESSER WRITER (a writer more like me) would have felt the need to articulate that paralysis, to dive into the dark abyss of this guy's soul, to replay the highlight reel of his maternal experiences, to grant him a flourish of defensive rage, or an aria of anguish.

That is so often our instinct as writers, and human beings: to render the inner life as a performance rather than a shared experience. Because, after all, we have all stood at the top of those stairs, have all stood in terror and sorrow and confusion before the enormity of the pain we risk—not as any function of misfortune or calculated assault—but simply by the miracle of our birth into this species.

We've already been shown everything we need to know about that man and all that he is carrying. Our job is simply to bear witness, to not to look away, to feel what we already feel.

THIS IS A RATHER WINDY WAY of saying something pretty simple: that it is the mission of all art, but literary art in particular, to engage with the inner life. And all I mean by the inner life is the private set of thoughts and feelings—of yearnings and fears and confusions—that are concealed from the world and yet persistently, unavoidably, experienced.

BECAUSE MY FOLKS WERE SHRINKS, I come by my preoccupation with the inner life honestly.

Here's a quick story about what it was like to grow up in my house, since you are wondering. One night at dinner, my older brother Dave started recounting this crazy dream. He was racing around his room because he was late for his job at Swensen's ice cream parlor. When he finally got to Swensen's, he found a fancy cocktail party in progress. He was handed a platter to carry around, with little dishes on it. Rather than ice cream, the dishes contained Russian dressing. At some point, Dave realized he was in his underwear, and was taken with a great humiliation.

We were all, like: *Weird dream, dude*.

"Freud talks about this," my dad said, "how some dreams contain puns."

"What pun?" Dave said.

"Well, you were late for work, so you didn't have time to put your pants on. There was a *rush in dressing*. Russian dressing."

MANY YEARS LATER, I worked as an investigative reporter. My job was to document the escapades of notable scoundrels, dirty cops, con men. But I kept pondering motive; what had possessed these people to self-destruct? "The interior life is a real life," as James Baldwin observes, "and the intangible dreams of people have a tangible effect on the world."

I decided to ship off to an MFA program where those intangible dreams could be exposed, examined, rendered into story. When I informed my boss of this plan, he glared at me for a good half minute. "You want to write *books*?" he said finally.

I didn't know what to tell him. I just had a hunch I'd been paying attention to the wrong part of the human arrangement.

A FEW MONTHS INTO THE PROGRAM, near the end of some drunken revel, a classmate asked if I'd ever read the novel *Stoner*. As a veteran stoner, I assumed the book would be devoted to the chronic arts. Not so. It begins:

William Stoner entered the University of Missouri as a freshman in the year 1910, at the age of nineteen. Eight years later, during the height of World War I, he received his Doctor of Philosophy degree and accepted an instructorship at the same university, where he taught until his death in 1956. He did not rise above the rank of assistant professor, and few students remembered him with any sharpness after they had taken his course.... Stoner's colleagues, who held him in no particular esteem when he was alive, speak of him rarely now; to the older ones, his name is a reminder of the end that awaits them all, and to the younger ones it is merely a sound which evokes no sense of the past and no identity with which they can associate themselves or their careers.

To understand how audacious I found this opening, you would have to know how loyal I was, back then, to the dogma of the MFA program, the smothering exhortations to *show, don't tell*. But it wasn't just the flat expository style of *Stoner* that flummoxed me. Williams had opened his novel by dryly announcing the insignificance of his protagonist. I assumed the point of literature was to document the lives of the lawless and lust riven. *Stoner* offered something altogether different: a dogged devotion to the inner life.

Perhaps for this reason, *Stoner* has regularly gone out of print, only to be resurrected by apostles like me. The author's own agent, Marie Rodell, thought the book was a loser.

I mention this not because I have a secret desire to humiliate literary agents—on the contrary, my desire to humiliate literary agents is quite public at this point—but because her assessment of the novel is so spectacularly wrongheaded. She fretted that *Stoner* would never sell because "its technique of almost unrelieved narrative is out of fashion."

In fact, it is the novel's narrative style that makes it so gripping. The book begins with that blunt little obituary, which has the effect of shifting the reader's curiosity away from Stoner's achievements and toward an accounting of his internal experience. What's less apparent, but just as crucial, is that this opening establishes a narrator capable of covering huge swaths of time and experience in a few sentences. This latitude allows the author, John Williams, to present the precise moments that wreak havoc on Stoner's inner life.

Two pages into the novel, Stoner's father proposes that his son leave their subsistence farm and go to college to study agriculture:

Never held with schooling when I was a young 'un. But now I don't know. Seems like the land gets drier and harder to work every year; it ain't rich like it was when I was a boy. County agent says they got new ideas, ways of doing things they teach you at the University. Maybe he's right. Sometimes when I'm out in the field I get to thinking.

Stoner's father is not someone who talks about his "inner life." But he does dream and fear and wonder. He knows his son is doomed if he doesn't do something. *Sometimes when I'm out in the field I get to thinking.*

Stoner arrives at college. In his required English course, a professor reads him a sonnet by Shakespeare and asks him to comment. Stoner can summon no words, but the world around him suddenly takes on a phantasmagoric intensity. "Light slanted from the windows and settled upon the faces of his fellow students, so that this illumination seemed to come from within them and go out against a dimness; a student blinked and a thin shadow fell upon a cheek whose down had caught the sunlight." Stoner marvels at the intricacy of his hands. He feels the blood flowing invisibly through his arteries. For several minutes after the others have left, he sits dazed. He wanders the campus, taking in "the bare gnarled branches of the trees curled and twisted against the pale sky." He regards his fellow students "curiously, as if he had not seen them before, and felt very distant from them and very close to them."

The compression of sensual and psychic detail makes this passage read like a reverie, though something quite simple is happening: literature has awakened him.

It's important to note this distinction: the rendering of the inner life isn't achieved by announcing to the reader that a character is *feeling* a lot. Such assertions of emotion register as mawkish. What happens is that characters start paying closer attention to the world around them, which inevitably reflects the world within them.

IN FACT, every few pages Stoner is slammed up against some harrowing realization, some impossible decision, some uncontainable urge. This relentless pacing is a direct result of the narration Rodell described as *unrelieved* and *out of fashion*.

As writers living in an age dominated by visual storytelling, our tendency is to conceive of drama in the way TV shows and movies do. The enduring lesson of *Stoner* is that the real action resides not in public confrontation but private reverberation. Here, for instance, is what happens when Stoner confesses to his mother that he won't be returning to the farm:

His mother was facing him, but she did not see him. Her eyes were squeezed shut; she was breathing heavily, her face twisted as if in pain, and her closed fists were pressed against her cheeks. With wonder Stoner realized that she was crying, deeply and silently, with the shame and awkwardness of one who seldom weeps.

He watches her for a moment more, then returns to his room, where he stares into the darkness above him. Later, after he buries his father, Stoner goes out to the fields and crumbles clods of dirt, watching the dry soil flow through his fingers. "He did not sleep; he lay on the bed and looked out the single window until the dawn came, until there were no shadows upon the land, until it stretched gray and barren and infinite before him."

We don't have to be told what Stoner is feeling in these moments. We are left to witness him, in essence, at the top of the stairs.

STONER'S MARRIAGE PROVES TORTUOUS, and his academic career is undone by a rival professor. He reaches a point where he begins to question whether he wishes to continue living. One snowy night, he turns out the lights in his office and listens to the silence, "the sounds that were absorbed by the delicate and intricately cellular being of the snow. Nothing moved upon the whiteness; it was a dead scene." He slips out of his own body and everything—"the flat whiteness, the trees, the tall columns, the night, the far stars"—appears tiny and far away, as if "dwindling to a nothingness."

This is the individual apprehended in a moment of pain so intense it triggers a cosmic disassociation. You don't have to be an English professor to hear the echoes here of Joyce at the end of "The Dead" ("his soul swooned slowly as he heard the snow falling faintly through the universe and faintly falling") or Frank O'Connor ("the old woman and the birds and the bloody stars were all far away, and I was somehow very small and very lonely").

I often point my students to this passage, as a demonstration of what I mean when I tell them *slow down where it hurts*. I stress this because our tendency in writing, and in life, is to do just the opposite, to hurry past our most abject moments, as if by doing so we might erase them from the record of our inner life. Williams doesn't run from the darkness within Stoner. He runs into that darkness.

Storytelling is not some mystical pursuit. It is mostly about building psychologically and emotionally reliable ramps to moments that matter and then slowing down. The reason is mechanical: if you cannot move the action forward, the writer's attention must turn in some other direction—inward, backward, or outward—toward a world that mirrors the one within.

STONER IS EVENTUALLY RESURRECTED by a brief and intense affair with a younger colleague, but the most enduring object of his love is his daughter, Grace, a quiet, thoughtful child whom he cares for and adores.

The most piercing tragedy of the book, therefore, is the manner in which Stoner's wife, Edith, essentially abducts Grace. She appears in the doorway of Stoner's study one evening and orders

Grace to leave. Stoner assures his wife the child is not bothering him. Edith ignores him and repeats her directive. Bewildered, Grace rises from her chair and walks toward the door. She pauses in the center of the room, "looking first at her father and then at her mother."

Once again: we don't have to be told what's happening inside Grace. We know that she's trying to figure out who's in charge, and, at the same time, imploring her father to rescue her.

He doesn't. Instead, Edith redesigns the girl's life in a manner inimical to her nature. Stoner tries to dodge the horror of what's happening. But Williams won't let him duck it. One day, he encounters Grace in the living room and they exchange shy smiles. Involuntarily, Stoner kneels and embraces his daughter. Her body stiffens. We can see instantly what's happened: she's become a hostage.

There are no histrionic fights or tearful reconciliations, just the brutal apprehension of the daughter he has surrendered by his cowardice: "She was, he knew—and had known very early, he supposed—one of those rare and always lovely humans whose moral nature was so delicate that it must be nourished and cared for that it might be fulfilled. Alien to the world, it had to live where it could not be at home; avid for tenderness and quiet, it had to feed upon indifference and callousness and noise."

As a dad, I can barely read this part of *Stoner* anymore.

I think of my youngest child, who does a lot of yelling and not much listening. Every week or so, he steps on someone's last nerve and that someone, often me, yells at him. At which point he crumbles. "Everybody hates me!" he'll wail. "Everybody wants me to die."

What's gutting about such moments is the sudden revelation of his fragility. Beneath all the bluster is a little person over-matched by the world of giants around him, painfully aware of the frustration he generates and scared he'll be abandoned.

Or I recall the epic tantrum our older son, Jude, threw after his uncle's wedding. He was so inconsolable that I eventually carried him upstairs to a little apartment above the reception area. "I want you to help me come down, Papa!" He kept howling these words at me.

I told him I couldn't bring him downstairs because he was too upset.

"I want you to help me come down! Help me come down, Papa!"

On and on it went until, to my horror, I snatched him up and hurled him onto a couch. "You're not going anywhere until you calm down!" I thundered. My son looked at me, mystified.

Instantly, I realized what he was actually saying to me, what he had been saying for the past half an hour: *I want you to help me* calm *down, Papa.*

THE POINT ISN'T THAT I'm a shitty dad. The point is that being a dad means dealing with the shitty parts—having to face the inner life of your kids, which they cannot hide and which you are often helpless to fix. My own lessons in helplessness have just begun. They'll stack up around me as my children pass into the world and shape their own fates, hand their hearts to the wrong people, suffer the arrows of outrageous fortune, chase their hopes into unseen hazards. To become themselves, our children will have to outgrow the people we imagine them to be, the ones we can keep safe. It is the fate of every parent therefore to gaze backward, like Stoner, at a lovely child who vanished long ago.

WHEN I FIRST READ *STONER*, twenty years ago, it was a book about literature as redemptive force. Then it was a novel about how to endure feuds, then one about the sacred work of teaching, the trials of marriage, then raising kids.

The last time I read *Stoner*, I should admit, it had become a book about mortality. It will come as no surprise that the closing pages of the book are a meticulous accounting of Stoner's death. At a certain point, as he lies dying, he ponders how others would view his life: "Dispassionately, reasonably, Stoner contemplated the failure that his life must appear to be. . . . He had dreamed of a kind of integrity, of a kind of purity that was entire; he had found compromise and the assaulting diversion of triviality. He had conceived wisdom, and at the end of the long years he had found ignorance. And what else? he thought. What else?"

Everyone harbors this merciless voice of judgment. It's the inevitable byproduct of a mind that measures worth using the math of the obituary, in which only the visibly heroic survives the final edit—life minus the inner life.

But something fascinating happens after Stoner's done pummeling himself. He falls into a slumber and wakes with his strength returned. He hears laughter and notices a trio of young couples cutting across his yard. "The girls were long-limbed and graceful in their light summer dresses, and the boys were looking at them with a joyous and bemused wonder. They walked lightly upon the grass, hardly touching it, leaving no trace of where they had been." Stoner is suffused with an abrupt joy, which signals the arrival of grace within the perishing body:

> He dimly recalled that he had been thinking of failure—as if it mattered. It seemed to him now that such thoughts were mean, unworthy of what his life had been.

HE DIMLY RECALLED *that he had been thinking of failure—as if it mattered.*

Has there ever been a more forgiving sentence written in the English language? It represents the eternal wish: that the arrival of death will cleanse our souls of the petty judgment by which we dishonor the miracle of our inner lives.

As someone who struggles with that petty judgment, someone who has dedicated his life, fitfully, to the transmission of love through the arrest of attention, someone who yearns openly for such a state of grace, I had been elated, always, to encounter this line. It was like the chunks of chocolate that used to drift to the bottom of the pints of mint chip ice cream I devoured on summer evenings long ago.

But a strange thing happened the last time I arrived at this line: I broke down sobbing. I broke down sobbing because I thought of my mother and the long, slow, unforgiving manner of her death.

As it should happen, my mother lived a life eminently worthy of praise. She was one of five women in the Yale Medical School class of 1960, scattered among eighty-five men, one of whom would become my father. During her residency, she gave birth to three children, all boys. Amid all this, she protested for civil rights, joined the anti-war movement, joined a commune and learned to weave on a loom, while also rising at 5 a.m. each morning to gather fresh eggs from the henhouse so that her sons would not starve. During my childhood, she saw patients all day, then raced home and got dinner on the table and did most of the household cleaning. She was, by any objective measure, a powerful and accomplished woman, a respected therapist, a brilliant pianist, a loving matriarch.

But there were moments when the strain showed. Sometimes, as she drove around on errands, she would forget we were in the backseat and I could hear her drift into addled soliloquy, whispered enumerations of all that weighed upon her. Or I would catch sight of her staring into the distance, shaking her head, as if making peace with the impossibility of her circumstance, or gathering for the next depredation.

She was bullied in our family, the unacknowledged victim of masculine privilege and the assumed healer of masculine doubt.

The problem was she didn't have any allies, really. It was all sons and patriarchs. When my older brother graduated from medical school, my mom called her father to share the good news.

"Well, Pop," she said, "we've got three doctors in the family now."

Her father paused. Then he asked, in genuine puzzlement: "Oh yeah, who's the third?"

My mother had by this time been a psychiatrist in private practice for twenty-five years and was training to become a psychoanalyst.

THE LAST DECADE of my mother's life was conducted under the shadow of calamity and illness. At some point, between her second and third cancers, she fell on the path outside her office. This fall had a curious effect. It sent her tumbling back to the Bronx of her childhood. She kept asking where her mother was. She was certain I was her uncle. Sometimes she would wake to find herself lying in a strange white room with needles and tubes taped to her arms. "Stevie," she would whisper. "I've just had the most terrible dream."

Along with much of her cognitive function, the boundary to her inner life had been breached. By the end of it, my mother had endured half a dozen bouts with cancers and chemo, two surgeries, radiation. All this "treatment" dulled her fierce intellect, impaired her work, and, toward the end, robbed her of reading and music, her last refuges.

Like many ambitious people, she experienced illness as a narcissistic injury. She blamed herself for being weak. At the same time, she could hardly acknowledge what was happening to her. Walking into her bedroom, one felt the smothering denial, the queasy code of silence that prevails when a group of people have agreed, tacitly and uneasily, to live within a frail dream. We couldn't talk about what was really happening. We couldn't say farewell.

There came a point, as in *Stoner*, where sickness took her hostage. She couldn't leave her room without the risk of collapse. We worried constantly that she would fall. One day, I came into her bedroom to check on her and saw that she had escaped her bed. Then I heard the splashing.

She had managed to get herself into the bath but lacked the strength to get herself out. It was left to my brother Dave and me to lift her from the tub and dry her skin and wipe away the trickles of blood from where she had tried to shave her legs. She was trembling violently the entire time, in tears, clutching at a towel, panicked at the thought that her sons would see her ravaged body. Her body looked beautiful. She looked like Eve.

I SHOULD ADMIT HERE that I felt a special burden, in part because I was living across the country as my mother died, but also because I saw us as perpetual allies: the family empaths, the left-handers, the readers. I had always known how vulnerable she was, beneath her indomitable energies, and I felt, in some secret part of myself, that it was my duty to make her happy, to dance the tango with her across the scuffed floors of our kitchen, to get her giggling when she was blue by imitating Harpo Marx.

It was agonizing to spend time with her at the end, because there was nothing I could do to quell her despair, to lure her back into the province of hope. I couldn't reach her, and, feeling helpless, I fled.

Every child probably thinks that he's the special one, so I'll admit that this is just my version of the story. But much later, at one of those dreadful gatherings where the guest of honor is missing, a young woman who had tended to my mother in her final weeks, when my father was too exhausted, took me aside. She told me that my mother had sat up at one point and looked around, suddenly alert. Then she had spoken a single word.

"Stevie?"

MY MOTHER LIVED AND DIED heroically by all accounts but the one that mattered: her own. Until the very end, she believed she was falling short. She lacked the strength to cook us meals, to come downstairs, to read stories to the kids, to drink her chocolate milkshakes. She was consumed not just by illness but by a sense of inadequacy. My mother deserved to die at peace with her inner life, like Stoner, to spend her final moments in that promised land. *She dimly recalled that she had been thinking of failure—as if it mattered.*

I HAVE TOLD YOU a number of personal stories about the inner life, but they are related to the larger story of our species, which is waging a sustained assault on the inner life.

To focus on the inner life today—to read books, to imagine with no ulterior agenda, to reflect on painful or confusing experiences—is to defy the clamoring edicts of our age, the buy messages, the endless pleas for followers and likes.

Writers have to find a different way of being in the world. The making of literature is the manner by which we come to understand our inner lives, by which we travel in difficult truth toward elusive mercy, and thereby reaffirm the bonds of human kindness.

I am speaking here of something that goes beyond the fate of our work, or the brief span of our lives. I am speaking of the man, or the woman, who stands in silence at the top of the stairs, just a few seconds longer, feeling the ghost of his beloved mother in his arms, rocking her back and forth, back and forth.

THE PRICE OF ENTITLEMENT
& THE WISDOM OF FAILURE

Early in my teaching career, I had one of those unsettling experiences that becomes, for a time, The Story You Tell at Parties. It involved a student—I'll call her Sara—who stalked me for weeks after receiving a B minus in my creative writing class. The department chair eventually forbade her from coming within one hundred yards of me, which left her to glare from the end of particularly long hallways. A few weeks into summer, I received my student evaluations. In the section marked Additional Comments, Sara had scrawled: *If writing was a part of my body, I would cut it off with an exacto knife.*

"And that was the best sentence she wrote all semester!" I announced to my fellow adjuncts, at those dreary parties.

We all laughed. We'd all had students who grade grubbed then exacted their revenge on evaluation forms. But mostly we laughed because these students represented a part of ourselves we wished to disavow, the part that obsessed over the editors who rejected *our* work and cursed the writers who were already more successful than we would ever be.

My behavior was despicable. I exploited a student's pain in a way that would have only confirmed her worst notions about the world of writing. Namely, that teachers in this world didn't just give you bad grades but mocked you behind your back. I also failed, rather abjectly, in creating the sort of safe workshop environment I was just preaching about. So I'm recalling all this at the bidding of a guilty conscience.

But I still think about Sara for another reason, too. Her story has come to represent an intractable problem in the teaching of writing: the problem of entitlement.

To understand what I mean, I need to tell you a little more about what transpired in our class. It's important to know that this was an undergraduate intro to creative writing class, so the students were all over the place in terms of experience and dedication. Sara arrived brimming with confidence. She made it known that she'd won literary awards in high school, and spoke frequently in class, sometimes a bit condescendingly.

It quickly became apparent that we approached storytelling differently. I wanted students to use simple, direct language, to resist performing on the page. For Sara, the point of writing was to show off her chops.

The story she turned in for the first workshop was full of garish metaphors and zany plot twists, and she marched into class expecting acclaim. As it happened, the other submission that day was a haunting and plainly autobiographical account of sexual coercion. The author, in contrast to Sara, looked terrified.

Over the course of the next hour, the energy in that room shifted. One story had transported us into the mind and body of a young woman on the brink of surrendering herself to a predatory older man; the other offered us little more than a writer eager for praise. The students were kind enough to Sara, but the contrast was impossible to miss; it came as a terrible humiliation to Sara.

She stopped speaking in class and gradually stopped completing assignments. I knew that she felt wounded by the workshop experience, but I had no idea how to reach her, so I gifted her a B minus and called it a day.

That summer, I received a bulky package from Sara, containing hundreds of pages of notes and drafts, every word she'd written for my class. I still have this dossier, two decades later. On every page, I can hear Sara insisting that I recognize her talent and devotion, that I remit her to the state of grace in which writing made her feel special. But a better grade wasn't going to get her there. She had abandoned humility and thrown in her lot with entitlement.

EVERY WRITER FIGHTS THE SAME BATTLE. We are constantly negotiating with ourselves, trying to bridge the gap between the disappointments we experience and the applause we covet. Entitlement is the little voice that assures us every rejection is an injustice, that the fault resides in our critics rather than our decisions.

It's an attitude that wears many disguises. A few years back, for instance, I overhead my MFA students deriding the *Best American Short Stories* anthology.

"Those stories are always great," I blurted out.

There was an awkward pause. Then one of my students asked if I was being ironic.

Readers can judge stories as they see fit, of course. But this wasn't a discussion about any particular story. It was a generalized contempt.

Here's what I suspect was really going on in that fiction workshop: My students were in a silent panic. Most of them had made significant sacrifices to attend graduate school. They were taking a big risk, financially and psychologically. And they were smart enough to recognize the steep odds against their ever placing a story in *Best American*. Rather than face the reality of their challenge—that they were going to have to spend thousands of hours working to improve *and* absorb tons of rejection *and* live in a state of economic and creative insecurity—they defaulted to a more convenient reality: that such anthologies are full of hacks whose inclusion (as one student later explained to me) boils down to nepotism.

This dynamic isn't unique to writers. Every graduate program in this country is filled with ambitious guppies who have no clue how big and cold the ocean really is. But the truth looming over students of writing—compared to those studying law or medicine or engineering—is that only a fraction will become published authors. Most will have to find other means of supporting themselves and their families.

The mounting competitive pressures on aspiring writers, along with the pace and ease of judgment fostered by digital technology, has amplified the problem of entitlement.

I'm not describing "snark" here. Snark is a conscious attempt to cast aspersion for narcissistic reward, a tool of self-promotion. Entitlement operates at an unconscious level. It's a defensive snobbery meant to keep feelings of failure at bay.

AND THAT'S THE WHOLE PROBLEM. Entitlement is the enemy of artistic progress because your essential task as a writer isn't to avoid failure but to learn from it. You have to be able to convert humiliation into humility. You have to be patient and stubborn enough to outlast your doubt. That means accepting setbacks as a part of the process.

I have an unfortunate wealth of experience in this area, because my central literary ambition—to write a novel worthy of publication—took me thirty years and five disastrous efforts. I was so consumed by this struggle that I wrote a short story about it. In "Larsen's Novel," our hero unexpectedly presents a novel manuscript to his best friend, who spends the rest of the story crafting far-fetched excuses to avoid reading it.

Not surprisingly, I had written a novel as wretched as Larsen's, which I had foisted upon a host of unlucky friends. This was, in fact, my third failed novel. I may be an extreme example of the genus, but I suspect that there are thousands of other writers whose desk drawers and hard drives harbor a "Larsen's Novel" or three. We're the biggest secret society in the literary world.

I've consistently defined myself as a failed novelist. I certainly don't recommend this self-appraisal to others, as it manages to

combine masochism with a strain of self-pity that is often nar-
cissism's tenant twin. But I do want to share the insight it took
me three decades to grasp: the failed novels have been central to
my success as a writer.

This success came, in each case, the moment I shifted from an
attitude of entitlement to one of acceptance and curiosity. Rather
than demanding why the world my couldn't see my genius, I
started to ask, *Why had these books failed?*

BEFORE I SHARE A FEW SPECIFIC LESSONS, I want to consider why writers are so quick to hide—and hide from—their
failures. My hunch is that it has to do with the intensely public
and competitive nature of publishing. I often think of us writers
as a legion of insecure siblings, all battling for the attention of a
few distracted parents, most of whom live in New York City and
won't return our emails. When one author enjoys success, the
rest of us get to watch them ascending through the fog of obscurity. We're exhorted to broadcast these triumphs via social media.
The net result is a zeitgeist that simultaneously compels us to
silence any mention of our failures while amplifying the shame
we feel about them.

I'm not advocating that writers spend years cheerfully pound-
ing away at futile projects. What I'm saying is that failure offers
us the chance to discern our self-defeating patterns.

My first two novels were about, respectively, an inept young
newspaper reporter and an inept adjunct professor. They sought

to mine the absurdities of the professional worlds I knew. But as often happens to writers early in their careers, the bromide *write what you know* became a trap. My narrator simply bumbled from one scene to the next, spouting smart-alecky commentary. The novels had no subtext, beyond: Aren't I clever?

It turns out that the crafting of what would now be called "auto fiction" requires a capacity for deep self-reflection. Novels such as Marguerite Duras's *The Lover* or Ocean Vuong's *On Earth We're Briefly Gorgeous* soar because their authors are engaged in an urgent search for the meaning of what they've lived through. I wasn't ready to do that work.

In the years I was composing my first two manuscripts, I wouldn't have been able to articulate any of this. I only knew that the books felt claustrophobic and muddling. Thus, for my third effort, I decided to write . . . a historical epic. In college, I had come across the story of Shabbatai Zvi, the most famous false messiah in Jewish history. I saw his tumultuous life as the ideal substrate for a novel and buried myself in research.

But novels can succeed only if authors are able to dramatize the upheaval *inside* their characters. And I had no idea how Zvi—a rabbi whose tortured psyche was shaped by arcane forms of mysticism—viewed the world. I just pushed the guy around the Levant, praying he might bump into the big-ticket items: love, loss, epiphany. He did not.

My fourth novel, set in the world of sports talk radio, linked the culture of fandom to the larger American project of militarism. The book had a serious purpose, a comic tone, and a compelling milieu. It also had a passive leading man. I overcorrected in my next novel, choosing as my hero a man of action who hurled himself into professional and libidinal entanglements at warp speed.

But velocity, as we've seen, isn't the same thing as direction. Reading over these two books recently, I recognized their shared flaw: a meandering plot. The scenes entertained but rarely instigated rising action. Nor had I recognized the central goal of all rising action, which is to dramatize the internal conflicts that besieged my heroes. My central job, it turned out, wasn't to engineer mayhem but to hurl my people toward self-revelation.

I'M PROVIDING A PITHY SUMMARY HERE, as if I skipped merrily from the failure to the helpful lessons, which is obvious bullshit. In fact, my initial reaction to each rejected manuscript was a lot like my student Sara. I didn't technically stalk anyone. But I begged various agents and editors to reconsider their assessments and raged at them when they wouldn't. In dire moments, I imagined gathering all my failed drafts into a dossier and mailing them out, as if by seeing all this work product some authority would award me the better grade of publication.

I'm not proud of these reactions. But over the years, I've come to see them as fairly reliable stations along the Arc of Entitlement. I note this because a certain degree of entitlement is a necessary part of the creative process. We have to feel entitled to tell our stories as writers, to make our voices heard. We're entitled to the effort, in other words, not the desired result.

It's worth interrogating what that desired result is, as well. Sara's troubles arose more from her motives than her aptitudes or efforts. She wanted her writing to prove she was worthy. The same can be said of my own endless struggle to write a novel.

As an insecure younger sibling whose parents worshipped Dickens and Austen, I had developed the conviction that I would rank as a True Writer only by publishing a novel. When a friend suggested that I didn't really want to write a novel, I fumed for months. But he was right. I didn't want to write a novel. I wanted to be a novelist. My ego was sucking up the attention my characters deserved.

And so, about five years ago, I gave up. I didn't stop writing. But I stopped staking my identity on my performance as a novelist.

Almost at once, an imaginative space opened within me. I began working on a story about two families—one rich, one poor—bound together by an alleged murder. I got stuck a lot. But I didn't panic because I was generally able to diagnose the problem from a previous failure. When the plot began to wander, I cut scenes. When the narrator's commentary became intrusive, I ditched it. I thought long and hard about the private schisms that tormented each character and how the plot might force these out into the open. For the first time in my life, I didn't push my characters through the story. They pulled me through it.

So I got my happy ending. It took me thirty years, but OK, that's how long it took. The outstanding question here, for me, is what became of Sara. Did she ever return to writing?

I owe her an apology. Because Sara wanted to learn. Even after that disastrous workshop, she came to my office hours. I tried to help her understand where her story felt too performative. But I should have focused more on *her*—on what writing meant to her and how to help her manage her feelings of disappointment. I should have recognized, as the workshop leader, that I had allowed competitive anxiety to infect our group dynamic, and that Sara was suffering because of it. If I could do it over, I would have tried to find a way to convey all this to Sara. I might even have shared a brief passage from the story I was writing that same term: "Larsen's Novel." At the very end of that piece, the friend who has been avoiding reading Larsen's novel speaks to Larsen's son, Jake:

> "Not anyone can write a book. Believe me. And your father's book doesn't suck, Jake. It's a good book. Not perfect. But nothing's perfect. Do you understand what I'm telling you? Nothing's perfect. That's not why we're here. We're here just to try. And do you know who wins, in the end, Jake? Who the winners are? The guys, like your father, who try. Those are the winners."

Or maybe I'd tell Sara about the silly internet video I've watched a hundred times or so—usually to avoid working on a novel. It shows a cat attempting to leap onto a nearby roof. Someone has drawn a set of equations above the cat's head, so that he appears to be calculating his precise angle and acceleration. Then he jumps and misses the roof and plummets out of the frame.

As a writer, I feel like that cat *all the time.* The reason I finally reached the roof wasn't because I got any stronger or improved my math. It was because I had become humbler before the enormity of my task, and thus more patient and self-forgiving. I finally wrote a decent novel—after three long decades—because I leaped from atop a mountain of my own failures.

TRUTH IS THE ARROW, MERCY IS THE BOW

HOW TO WRITE THE UNBEARABLE STORY

When I was ten, my parents shipped me and my brothers off to stay with a babysitter for the weekend. They did this every few months, because we fought *a lot*. The babysitter's name was Kay Brennan. She drove us south an hour, in her rumbling Barracuda, to Hollister, California, where she lived with a pack of unruly Belgian sheep dogs. Kay smoked menthols and listened to a lot of Stevie Nicks. There wasn't much for us to do in Hollister. Our go-to activity was to whack clods of dirt with an aluminum baseball bat in the empty field behind Kay's bungalow. We loved the impact, the ping of the pebbles in those clods.

One morning, it was my turn with the bat. My older brother Dave was standing behind me. I knew this. I had been warned. I reared back anyway. I've never forgotten the sensation of that bat striking my brother's face, the spongy crack of it, the red geyser of his mouth.

I worshipped my older brother. I would have done anything for the least scrap of his praise. But he was often cruel toward me. That's why I swung the bat. I carried this version of the story around for decades, composing a series of mawkish poems in commemoration, one of which, eventually, I sent along to Dave. I was hoping for absolution, obviously.

A week later, Dave called to tell me I had gotten the story all wrong. He had known I was swinging the bat and been told to back off repeatedly. Dave's testimony is that he stepped into the path of my swing. Some part of him felt guilty for how mean he was to me. This was the punishment he chose.

Who can say, in the end, which version is the truth?

The truth is the blood.

The truth is the scar that still marks Dave's upper lip, a pale crescent.

I often tell this story to writing students, in an effort to distinguish between fiction and creative nonfiction. The latter, I tell them, is a radically subjective version of events that objectively took place. You're allowed to make things up, but we have a name for that. It's called fiction. You have to be honest with the reader about the nature of your work.

But there's another way to frame this story: as an act of seizure. What I'm doing, after all, is seizing the right to share with the world *my* version of this episode, in which Dave plays the guilt-ridden bully to my spurned younger sibling. My parents come off as negligent. And there's Kay Brennan, puffing on a

Kool, smelling of dog. By assuming the right to narrate, I become the boss, the final arbiter of our family history. If anyone else were doing the telling, it would be a different story.

It's no surprise I assumed this role. I'm a white guy who grew up in a middle-class home with two loving parents who may have taken the odd weekend off but nurtured all their children and made them feel seen and heard. Beyond the confines of our home, I've moved through a world that has been sending me the message, every day and in a million different ways, that my story matters and that I have every right to tell it.

But now imagine—perhaps you don't have to—that you were born in a female body, a body of color, an immigrant body, a disabled body, a body reared in poverty, a gay body, a trans body, a neurodiverse body. Imagine moving through a world that regards your voice as marginal, defective, or even dangerous, a world indifferent to, or outright hostile toward, the story you might want to tell.

Imagine you were born into a family with only one parent, or no biological parents. Imagine coming of age in a family haunted by divorce, trauma, addiction, mental illness, incarceration. Imagine a home marked by emotional violence, or physical violence, or sexual abuse. Imagine the internalized sense of shame and secrecy.

Every family enforces its own codes of silence. And every writer is, in this sense, violating some kind of omertà. But the scale of these prohibitions operates on an inverse relationship. The greater the resistance to the telling of a particular story, the greater the value in its being told.

—————

I'm THINKING NOW OF THE STUDENT I met a few years ago, at a writing conference in Florida. She was a junior in college, majoring in business if I'm remembering right, a beautiful, nervous young woman who took a creative writing class as her elective and had thus been roped into a manuscript consultation with me.

She had written a comic essay about getting her hair styled as a girl at a cut-rate salon. This was a big deal to her parents, who didn't have a lot of money and who recognized their daughter's beauty as vital to her prospects. I won't go into details here, because the story is ultimately hers to tell. But I will say that glints of despair kept showing through her antic descriptions, moments when this grooming ritual sounded more like torture.

I didn't say any of this to her. Mostly, I stuck to line edits. But I did make one comment of a personal nature. "It seems like there was a lot of pressure on you to be perfect."

At this, the young woman, whom I had met only a few minutes earlier, whose hair looked worthy of a shampoo commercial, began to weep in quiet convulsions.

This is what I've witnessed as a teacher, over and over. People come to writing as a way of going in search of themselves. They are trying to process volatile feelings that went unexpressed in their families of origin, to revisit unresolved traumas. They are writing about what they can't get rid of by other means.

This is not to discount an ecstatic devotion to language, or the transformative powers of imagination. But I'm talking about motives.

Herein lies the question every writer faces, at some level: Is my compulsion to tell the truth stronger than my fear of the consequences?

WHAT MOST WRITERS DO is disguise the truth. Some use the comic impulse to defang their pain, like the young woman I met in Florida. Others decide, rather abruptly, to convert their memoirs into novels, which they hope will grant them distance and plausible deniability. Fiction writers frisk the world for symbolic versions of their experience.

Years ago, for instance, I went to visit an old friend in Maine. I wanted to meet his newborn daughter, and to offer condolences for his mother, who had died a few months earlier. My friend greeted me at the door and introduced me to his father, who was hovering near the kitchen island. I expected to make a little small talk before proceeding to the baby, whom I could see in the next room, curled on her mother's lap.

But when my friend's father learned that I was an adjunct professor, he launched into an odd reminiscence. Years ago, when he was an adjunct, the president of his university had called him late one night to tell him that one of his students had been killed in a car accident. They needed to notify the next of kin. Would he be willing to identify the body?

I could understand why a widower's thoughts would drift toward a death memory. But it struck me that he was also nervous, uncertain how to connect with his family in the absence of his wife. When I got home, I sat down at the keyboard. In a matter of hours, I had written my version of the episode, changing a few details but remaining faithful to its essence.

Some years later, this story found its way into in my debut collection. My father wrote me a kind letter about that book, graciously ignoring its pornographic content. He reserved special comment for the story about the widower, the one I've been telling you about. "I never realized I was so emotionally distant as a father," he wrote.

I remember rearing back from the page in alarm. I wanted to call him immediately, to correct the record: *Wait a sec, Dad, that story's not about . . .*

But of course it was. That's why it had snagged in my mind, why the fictionalized version had come reeling out of me. I'd felt too guilty, and too loyal, to write about this version of my dad, so my unconscious had latched on to a story that did the dirty work for me.

That's how it works with fiction: our inventions are veiled confessions. Our job isn't to figure out why we're writing a particular story. It's to trust our impulses and associations, to pay attention to our attention.

THE REASON YOU SIT DOWN to write any story—beyond your ego needs—is because you want to tell the truth about some part of your life that haunts you. If the story is any good, you're going to reach places of distress and bewilderment. You're going to name names, shatter silences, wake some ghosts. There's a lot of exposure involved. And thus, a lot of ambivalence.

Writing is an attention racket. But it's also a forgiveness racket. The best way to keep going when the anxiety of exposure strikes is to remember that your goal is to forgive everyone involved, yourself foremost. A great story, of whatever sort, is not a monument to sorrow or destruction. It is a precise accounting of the many ways in which our love gets distorted, a secular expression of spiritual forbearance.

Many years ago, I got invited to the Sewanee Writers' Conference. It was my first big jamboree and I'm sure I strutted around making a fool of myself. But the only thing I really remember of that conference is Barry Hannah's reading.

I was a devout fan. "My head's burning off and I got a heart about to bust out of my ribs." That was the first line of his I ever read, and I never looked back. I read his collection *Airships* chronically, and though his stories were loose and Southern and baroque (nothing like mine), they had helped me come out of the closet as an emotionalist.

Folks at Sewanee still loved to tell tales about Barry's wild days. But he was into his sixties by then, slowed by cancer, soft-spoken, even shy, and leathery as a lizard, with a deep croaking voice that made all his words sound as if they came from the pulpit.

I can't remember the story he read, only that it involved a friend of the narrator's getting into some kind of fatal mayhem. What I do remember is how Barry paused, toward the end of the piece, and how we in the audience, after a few moments of confusion, recognized what was happening, that Barry Hannah was weeping, that the memory of his friend, and of his friend's death, had overtaken him.

"I'm sorry," he said quietly, touching at a tear on his cheek. "I didn't realize all that would come up."

It was a profound moment for me, because, like many of his readers, I hadn't really grasped that there was an actual person behind the authorial persona (Barry the Drinker, the Madman, the Legend). He wasn't just dreaming up escapades in some haze of whiskey and genius. He was writing about the people he had lost.

Barry himself was, I'm sure, quite embarrassed. But there was nothing he could have read, or taught us, that would have delivered the message more plainly: your job as a writer is to love and to mourn, to tell the unbearable story so that others might feel less alone in theirs.

ALL OF WHICH SOUNDS excruciatingly noble. But it's hard to hold on to when your story involves a violent partner, a sexual assault, a murderous impulse toward a child.

Or how about an abusive parent? To write truthfully about such a figure is to wrench open a portal of pain. Rather than healing a rift, the act of writing—regardless of genre—can reopen old wounds. And that's what often happens, frankly, at least in initial drafts.

I recently read a memoir by a student whose adoptive mother was a genuinely destructive force, negligent and controlling, verbally mocking and physically menacing.

But there were aspects of this mother's history—briefly noted—that struck me as vital. She had been raised in an aristocratic family, primarily by servants, with no real sense of maternal attachment. A violent revolution forced her family to move when she was young, and they lost their fortune. She married for love, against her family's wishes, and her husband promptly moved her halfway across the world to a small town in the United States. She couldn't speak English and had no support. So she sat alone in a dim apartment, while her husband pursued his career. Then she discovered that she couldn't conceive children, a source of extreme shame in her culture. Long before she adopted children, she was battling profound mental health issues, which went untreated and thus drove her deeper into isolation.

None of this context excuses the cruelty inflicted on her daughter. But taken together—truly acknowledged, that is—these facts allow us to reckon with the author's mother as someone whose cruelty arose from despair. Instead, the memoir was dominated by scenes of maternal tyranny.

Vengeance is a natural impulse when you relate the story of a damaging figure in your life. But the reader always sniffs it out. It's the difference between an indictment and a trial, between a rant and a lamentation. When I'm telling stories of this kind, I always try to challenge my instincts, to adopt the perspective of my antagonists, to complicate my version. I try to figure out if my criticisms are a form of projection. That is, if I'm angry at someone else because I'm guilty of the same transgression.

Claiming the role of storyteller doesn't give us a franchise on the truth. Indeed, it may trigger feelings of grandiosity that flatten out those around us. Most difficult of all, we have to tell the parts of the story that we are most apt to hide, even from

ourselves: that our antagonist was sometimes kind and even tender to us, that we once clung to them with a fierce loyalty, that
they proved too weak and damaged to protect us, that beneath
all the swirling rancor is an ache that binds us together.

It is, of course, unrealistic to expect a traumatized child to
summon forgiveness toward an abusive parent. But the writer's
task as an adult, looking back on those wounding events, is to
tell the whole truth, and that pursuit is doomed without forgiveness. The more mercy you can summon, the deeper you will
travel into truth.

FOR MANY YEARS I was reluctant to tell my girlfriends I was in
love with them. I viewed *love* as a code word for certain emotional promises I had little hope of keeping, and therefore made
the typically scuzzy masculine argument that "love" was an arbi-
trary threshold, who really knew what it meant, and what mattered was how I behaved, not the terms affixed to those
behaviors. This was the part of the story just before I got
dumped.

I still think of *love* as a fuzzy word. But as a storyteller, I've
come to see love in more precise terms, as *an act of sustained
attention implying eventual mercy.* There is nothing more dis-
heartening to me than a story in which the writer expresses
contempt for his characters. It's the one posture I can't abide,
because it amounts to a conscious rejection of art, whose first
and final mission is the transmission of love.

That's what's happening when you read any great piece of writing: the love transmitted from the author to her characters is being transmitted to you, the reader. This is why I exhort students to love their characters at all times.

I don't mean by this that you should coddle them. On the contrary, it is your sworn duty, as a fiction writer, to send your characters barreling into danger. And, as a nonfiction writer, to witness and interrogate their darkest deeds. Nor do I mean to endorse some bland form of moral absolution. I mean something more much like what the authors of the New Testament ascribe to Jesus Christ. That you love people not for their strength and nobility but, on the contrary, for their weakness and iniquity. Your job is not to burnish the saint but to redeem the sinner.

I want to emphasize this because certain agents and editors stress that characters should be *likable*, which, along with its ditzy cousin *relatable*, is one of those marketing words that has infiltrated publishing. (Thanks, capitalism!)

I implore you not to think of your characters in this way. Your job is to reveal them as they are, not to charm the audience. It is both fraudulent and deeply condescending to assume that readers will turn away at the first disturbing utterance or action from your heroine.

To me, the appearance of a "likable" character triggers the same exhausted skepticism with which I greet certain social media posts, the ones where everyone is smiling and the food is backlit. Such airbrushed displays offer me nothing to participate in, other than envy.

Back in 2014, Claire Messud published *The Woman Upstairs*. The heroine, a forty-year-old teacher named Nora Eldridge, has retreated from her creative ambitions into a life of stifled duty. The novel is an epic rant, delivered by a woman angry enough to "set the world on fire."

While promoting the book, Messud was interviewed by a young female critic, who asked her a rather loaded question: "I wouldn't want to be friends with Nora, would you? Her outlook is almost unbearably grim."

"For heaven's sake, what kind of question is that?" Messud responded. She went on to catalogue the many despicable leading men in our canon, before adding: "If you're reading to find friends, you're in deep trouble. We read to find life, in all its possibilities. The relevant question isn't 'Is this a potential friend for me?' but 'Is this character alive?'"

Characters such as Nora refuse to be stuffed in an attic or kept silent any longer. (I'm thinking, too, of Antoinette from *Wide Sargasso Sea*, and her final declaration, before she burns Thornfield to the ground: "Then I turned round and saw the sky. It was red and all my life was in it.")

For the record, Nora's outlook isn't unbearably grim. It's unbearably *honest*. She's furious at the lost promise of feminism, but also at her own acquiescence. "I always thought I'd get farther," she confesses. "I'd like to blame the world for what I've failed to do, but the failure—the failure that sometimes washes over me as anger, makes me so angry I could spit—is all mine, in the end." She goes on, "Isn't that always the way, that at the heart of the fire is a frozen kernel of sorrow that the fire is trying—valiantly, fruitlessly—to eradicate."

The Woman Upstairs is a stark example of the work literature is meant to do, which is to implicate the reader, to bring them into contact with the damaged precincts of their inner life, to help them feel less isolated with those parts of themselves. Big emotions are disruptive to our lives off the page, which is why we expend so much energy hiding our sadness, suppressing our rage, dodging conflict, striving to be likable.

As writers, we have to accept a different code of conduct. Our mission is to aim for the painful events and unresolved feelings, to spend time amid desperate characters, to push past our inhibitions. It takes work for us to find a voice capable of such courage.

Vivian Gornick writes about the process as a form of liberation. For years, she sought a narrator who could tell the truth as she alone could not. "I longed each day to meet again with her. It was not only that I admired her style, her generosity, her detachment (such a respite from the me that was me); she had become the instrument of my illumination."

It is my own sentimental belief that writers justify what we do by exhibiting superhuman compassion in the face of persistent misbehavior. Our books are the written record of that compassion, but they shouldn't be confused with our lives. Off the page, I am often a shithead: insecure, controlling, tiresome. Just ask my wife.

That's the ultimate dividend of writing: you get to be a better person on the page than you are the rest of the time. More merciful and therefore more honest.

———————

WRITERS FIND A LOT OF EXCUSES to avoid exposure, especially early in our careers, especially if we've been told to remain quiet. One way is by leaping ahead to the part of the story where we're already published and everyone is mad at us. But exposure is something that's incremental, something we get to control.

Setting down an unbearable story in a private draft isn't the same as submitting it to a workshop, or publishing it, or showing it to a beloved. Those acts are further downstream. Self-assertion comes first.

I experienced this for four years, as the cohost of the *Dear Sugars* podcast. My friend Cheryl Strayed and I received thousands of letters from people in crisis, as many as a dozen a day. Very few of our correspondents were writers. But Cheryl and I were struck by the sheer, unflinching beauty of the prose.

We could see the precise spots where the stories faltered, where the author descended into self-pity or contempt or fraudulence, where a deficit of mercy kept them from reaching some agonizing final truth. That was where we came in, I guess.

Most of what we told our listeners they knew already. They knew they needed to set a boundary. They knew love was supposed to feel safe. They knew it was time to leave. What they needed, most of the time, wasn't wisdom, but permission. We might have helped around the margins, but Cheryl and I weren't even the crucial part of the equation. It was the very act of composing and sending those letters—of granting themselves the right to tell their own story—that was healing.

TRUTH IS THE ARROW, MERCY IS THE BOW

What we're really afraid of is facing the truth, living in the pain and confusion of it. But grace arrives only when you're standing in the truth.

I'VE WRITTEN THIS ESSAY so many times. I keep finding reasons to cut the story I told you at the beginning, the one about hitting my brother Dave in the face with a baseball bat. It makes my childhood—which was one of extraordinary privilege and relative safety—sound dangerous, and therefore sensational. It's not even something that happened to me.

So out it went.

Then I put it back again.

Why?

Because, I think, some part of me is still ten years old, in that dirt field in Hollister, still in love with my big brother, still angry at him for not loving me back. Maybe by telling the story I get to smash Dave all over again, this time for a bunch of strangers.

Or maybe the truth is even worse, because I know what comes next, all the ways in which Dave struggles later on, succumbs to the bad chemistry coursing through him, calls me with his brain on fire, from somewhere beyond the reach of my good fortune, muttering strange theories, quoting the haunted movies of our youth, repeating himself, falling short of the God I still need him to be. Maybe I'm still trying to take the blame for those struggles.

I haven't figured it out.

I only know that Dave and I have managed, after many years of estrangement, to find a path back to one another. We're both the worse for wear, often exhausted, but also properly humbled, able to be kind in a way that once felt impossible. It has been one of the great honors of my life to help reinvent our brotherhood, to call him a friend.

Once upon a time there were two brothers who could be intimate only through an act of violence. I don't want to go back there. But I still remember how it felt the old way: the weight of that bat, the spongy crack. It's fine to be scared, maybe even necessary. The path to the truth runs through shame but ends in mercy. We've all got work to do.

PART IV

FAQ

Q: *What is your writing process?*

A: Many bongs ago, a Famous Writer came to visit my MFA program. His book of stories had just won the Pulitzer Prize, so he was arriving, really, from Planet Fame, a place we could see at night, flickering in the vault of heaven. At some point during his visit, the Famous Writer informed us that he wrote for at least four hours every day. This length of time was the bare minimum necessary for him to reach the spiritual plane upon which he could commune with his characters. His tone was resonant, faintly Buddhist. For the next decade or so—between bouts of Writer's Block—I wrote for at least four hours every day. I produced two excruciating novels and many excruciating stories. Mostly, I sat in misery, watching the large, industrial clock I'd stolen from the university library. 3:41. 3:47.

I understand the urge to shake down more established writers for their trade secrets. But your process belongs to you. Do a self-inventory. When and how do *I* write best? Early mornings? Late nights? Long stretches or short bursts? Coffee or wine? Think about the circumstances that prevailed when you composed your truest work. Seek to replicate them. This will require management. You have to design your schedule to protect those windows.

As your life changes, your process will change. When I was a single dude, I could spend hours staring at stolen clocks. Now I have three children and a partner with her own creative needs, and bigger bills to pay, and less energy, less bandwidth. That may sound like a set of complaints. It's really just a list of conditions. I have to be more focused and enforce clear boundaries around my creative time. My wife and I have to flee the clamor of our home to do sustained work. We take turns.

I can't control whether the muse will visit or not. Neither can you. Your goal isn't to attain some mystical state. It's simply to show up, as best you can, to put yourself in a position to make decisions at the keyboard.

Q: *When am I allowed to call myself a Writer?*

A: Whenever you like. The question itself, though, suggests a yearning for legitimacy. My advice is to avoid the noun and emphasize the verb. Like any other title, the noun links to status, thus hierarchy, thus ego. I still avoid telling people I'm a writer. It sounds presumptuous, like I should carry a feather quill. Those are my hang-ups, of course. If you find it empowering to identify yourself as a writer, go for it.

I prefer the term *Word Decider*, which describes the activity rather than the identity. It's kind of nerdy, and only a partial description—we are also plot deciders, syntax deciders, character deciders—but if I ever print up a business card, that's the phrase I'll plunk beneath my name. *Word Decider*.

Q: *Can you recommend a literary agent?*

A: Once upon a time, an agent wrote me out of the blue, to solicit a piece for a rather silly anthology. I asked how much he could pay. Alas, he responded, there was no money in it for contributors. So who *is* getting paid, I wondered. Our email correspondence continued for a while, in that murderously polite manner that prevails when one party refuses to answer simple questions. Eventually, the agent admitted that he and his coeditor had received a $50,000 advance. Any payment over $500 would put them in the red, he argued, and any payment under $500 "would be pointless."

I'm telling you this story to emphasize that writers and agents live in different worlds. The writer is an artist. The agent is a broker. I understand why writers place so much stock in acquiring an agent. It's a vote of confidence and a badge of legitimacy in a realm fraught with rejection and insecurity. Securing representation is not a ticket to the dance, though. It's the beginning of a process by which your art is brought to market.

An agent offers expertise and connections. They also add another layer of emotional bureaucracy to the submission process. Rather than worrying about not hearing from editors, you get to worry about not hearing from your agent. The whole system is predicated on keeping writers in the dark. Agents and publishers don't want us to take on the burdens of negotiation, or learn too much about our own contracts, or pitch editors directly.

Ideally, agents do more than broker. They serve as advocates, editorial advisors, even business managers. They earn that 15 percent. But no agent is going to pluck you from obscurity. That will be accomplished by your hard labor, all the tough, beautiful decisions you made alone in some room. Remember that. Hold on to it.

Q: *What's your stance on simultaneous submission?*

A: It's irresponsible to submit work to more than one magazine/editor/agent, if the recipient forbids multiple submissions. But also: you, the writer, have invested a lot more time in your work than they have. It's understandable that you don't want to wait months for a single rejection before you submit again. This was how I rationalized sending out multiple submissions back in the day.

So I don't have a hard-and-fast rule here.

But I do want to note the power dynamics around submission, because—as the name implies—it's the process where you, the control-freak author, lose control.

RULE ONE: Don't send out a draft. You're asking someone with a giant stack of manuscripts to invest in your work.

RULE TWO: Disappointment is the essential risk. Your ego, and your faith, may take a hit. Be real about that, especially if you're feeling fragile.

RULE THREE: You probably won't get closure. Rejection usually means a form letter, or a set of bromides.

RULE FOUR: You cannot win if you don't buy a ticket.

Back in grad school, I published a few stories in literary journals, and made sure everyone knew. What I never confessed was that I'd received a hundred rejections for every acceptance. The only other person in our program who knew this was the poet and essayist Camille Dungy, who house-sat for me one summer and received my mail. Camille has told this story for years. The reason I got my work published wasn't because I was a better writer than my comrades. It was because I bought more tickets.

RULE FIVE: All you can control is your decisions and (on good days) your reactions. The world decides the rest.

Q: *Does withholding information build suspense?*

A: The simplest way to answer this is by explaining the difference between surprise and suspense. To do so, I'm going to steal a riff from my pal, the novelist Bruce Machart.

OK. Let's say you have the poor fortune of being enrolled in one of my workshops. I walk in to class on the first day and run my mouth for three hours. Then, at the very end of class, I pull a paintball gun from my satchel and shoot you in the face.

Surprise!

But let's say, on the other hand, that I walk into class on that first day and open my satchel and pull out the paint gun and set it on my desk and say, "One of you is going to trigger me today. It happens every class, I'm afraid. And when it happens, I'm not going to scowl at you, or make a note in my grade book. I'm going to wait till the end of class and then pick up this paintball gun and, in front of everyone, blast you in the face."

Now ask yourself: In which version of the class am I going to pay closer attention? The first one, in which the calamity comes as a shock? Or the second one, in which you are apprised of the risk upfront? *That*'s the difference between surprise and suspense.

Q: *Is it ever OK to confuse the reader?*

A: Yes. If your protagonist is confused, for instance. The reader should *participate* in that confusion. The sworn enemy here is confusion that prevents the reader from understanding, and thus participating in, the world of the characters.

When I was editing a literary magazine, this was the most common reason we rejected stories—because we were lost. "Where are we?" we asked ourselves. "What's going on? Who's telling this story? What's in it for them?" We spent the pivotal early moments struggling to orient ourselves, rather than bonding with the characters. Then we gave up.

Q: *It seems like you think* show, don't tell *is a crock. True?*

A: Imagine you're embarking on a new short story. Because you've learned that stories are most compelling in scene, you begin with a man and woman entering a tall building from opposite directions. Better yet, to keep the reader from getting bored, you start with the man and the woman standing before a bank of elevators.

They're middle-aged, formally dressed. There's a nervous little ballet as they enter the elevator, and another one over who's going to press the buttons. They're both headed for the penthouse suite on the thirty-ninth floor, which traps them in the same small space, as Hitchcock recommends. Because you've taken your Show-Don't-Tell multivitamin, you're able to record lots of telling details. The dark patches beneath the woman's eyes, discernible despite the concealer she's applied. The sidelong glances the man casts at her every few seconds. How he reaches to loosen his collar. Even the drop of sweat that rills down the woman's torso and traces her ribs. One senses a tremendous, suppressed tension between these two.

Let's consider another approach. In this version, you begin by telling the reader about two high schoolers who hang out in adjacent cliques. The dude's family has money, so the young woman thinks of him as stuck up. She's in AP classes, so he sees her as an intellectual snob. There's a lot of sarcastic combat, the kind meant to disguise the spark they both feel.

Along comes prom night. Ah, prom night! Long on boozy banter, short on discretion. Our couple wind up on some dark terrace making out. It's quite a scandal, because he's already got a girlfriend, or she does. (It's your story. You get to decide.)

Off they go to college. But a few summers later, at some backyard party, they meet again. They've grown up enough to hate themselves a little less, and the moment comes when they summon the nerve to stare into each other's eyes and acknowledge the spark.

They court, marry, build careers. Then they have kids, one after another, a girl and a boy. On their tenth anniversary, they head off to an eco-lodge and suddenly—oops—there's another baby on the way. For their fifteenth anniversary, they decide they deserve something special. So they go for it: an in-ground pool. Why not? The big kids love to swim; the little one is half dolphin. Cavorting in the pool is about the only thing that tires her out, even if she needs to be reminded to wear her water wings.

At some point, the wife heads out of town for the weekend. Or maybe it's the husband. Point is, there's only one parent to handle meals and soccer games and emails from work. And at some point, amid all the hubbub, the gate to the pool gets left open. And the third child—the little girl who needs reminding about her water wings—wanders through that gate, alone.

Now then: nobody can truly know the depth of this kind of loss. We can say only that this couple is living in a very different story now. They love each other. They've built a life of deep meaning and joy, so they put everything they can into staying connected. The wife refuses to blame the husband. The husband struggles not to blame himself. They both get into therapy, then couple's counseling. They do the work.

But gradually, inexorably, it becomes clear that they can no longer live together under the shadow of this loss. They promise each other that they'll separate without rancor or blame. But you know how it goes: hurt people hurt people.

They spend a year keeping the marriage alive through legal combat. But eventually the day comes when they have to finalize the divorce. It's the second hardest thing they've ever faced, to give up on the dream of reconciliation, to sign away all they've built. One of them has hired a fancy lawyer, so they have to go to a fancy office to make it official. In the end, they wind up entering the same tall building from opposite directions. They wind up in front of the same bank of elevators. The papers are waiting for them, neatly arrayed on a conference table on the thirty-ninth floor. The only way to get there is by taking the elevator.

You simply can't tell me that the first ride we took in that elevator is the same as this ride. Because now, every detail we're shown—the nervous ballet over who presses the buttons, her sleepless eyes, his desperate tugs at the shirt collar, even that lonely drop of sweat—arises from the truth of what they're living through.

I'm not suggesting this kind of essential context can't be revealed, skillfully, thrillingly, in the midst of scenes. Or that we should discard the Show-Don't-Tell mantra. When our characters are in danger, our readers want (and deserve) scenes, not narrative assertions. But be generous in revealing the danger. Tell the reader just enough that they can *feel what they're being shown.* When you trap your characters in an elevator, make sure the reader knows what they're carrying across the threshold.

Q: *Should my writing make money?*

A: Your motives are your own, of course, as are your circumstances. But to the extent possible, I advise you to uncouple artistic creation from financial expectation. The voices in your head when you write should be helping you tell the story, not sell it.

Q: *How much do titles matter?*

A: A shit ton. Titles are the first *indication* of your story's thematic concerns, an *initiation* into its tone, and an *inducement* to keep reading. They are the face of your work.

The title story in Karl Iagnemma's luminous collection *On the Nature of Human Romantic Interaction* not only introduces us to his protagonists—mathematicians and scientists—but captures their frantic and fruitless efforts to quantify the chaos of love. Samantha Irby called her uproarious essay collection *Wow, No Thank You* to convey her raw, self-deprecating style, and her gently bemused attitude toward life.

Raymond Carver's editor switched the title of his most famous story from "The Beginners" to "What We Talk About When We Talk About Love." It was the right call, because the latter does so much more work. It's colloquial and unremitting in the exact same way as the story, which is one long, drunken rant about the inherent perils of marriage. It also passes what I call The TOC Test: If you came across the title in a table of contents of a literary magazine, would you be intrigued enough to turn to that page?

A final criterion: inimitability. Is the title in question charged with the linguistic and thematic energies of your piece? Is it that specific and precise? I can't tell you how dispiriting it is when an author mails in her title, when it relies on a cliché or an overwrought symbol, or employs a pun, or parrots the last line of the story.

The best titles arise organically, from the language of the piece in question, usually in the form of a phrase that evokes multiple meanings.

Remember my brilliant student Ellen Litman? Years ago, she turned in a short story about a family of Russian immigrants newly arrived to America. Her original title was something like "How to Survive in America." As we discussed the piece in workshop, we kept returning to a scene in which the narrator's father, set adrift in a vast American supermarket, clutches a chicken "like it was the last chicken in America." This image encapsulated the story: its blend of black humor and pathos, of desperation and courage. Not only did the story get a new name, but (at her instigation) it became the title of her debut novel.

Most of what keeps writers from finding great titles is embarrassment. They view titles as a form of advertising for a product they don't quite believe in yet. But titles aren't just some billboard slapped above the text. The search for a title should draw you deeper into the mysteries of your work. It's a promise you're making to *yourself* as well as the reader.

Q: *Can my first draft be a mess?*

A: Yup. The first one is for you. It's your chance to shake down your unconscious, to see what comes loose and what sticks, to take chances, to duck down blind alleys, to get lost.

Q: *How much research should I do?*

A: Enough to bring us inside your characters—and not one iota more.

The qualifier is crucial, because you may be tempted to hide in your research, hoping that if you just "do your homework," the people in your stories will come alive. That's not how it works. Your research should be directed by who your characters are, what they desire and fear, how they see the world.

Maggie O'Farrell's 2020 novel *Hamnet* is spellbinding not because she vividly portrays Elizabethan England, but because she brings us inside the sensual, lived experience of our protagonist, Agnes Shakespeare. We smell, taste, touch the domestic and botanical realms central to her role as mother and healer, while, in a welcome twist, her famous husband remains offstage, tending to his plays in London.

During one virtuosic passage, O'Farrell traces the transmission of bubonic plague from a flea-infested monkey in Alexandria, Egypt, all the way to the Shakespeare homestead in Warwickshire. This meticulous viral accounting presages the tragedy at the heart of the novel: the death of Agnes's son, young Hamnet. O'Farrell wears her research so lightly it doesn't feel like research at all. It's just a remarkable tale.

This applies equally to nonfiction projects. If you're writing a memoir set in a country that has undergone social and political upheaval, that history is an integral part of the story. If you're going to write a book questioning the morality of football, as I did some years ago, you had better get your facts straight. Curiosity should serve a devotion to the truth.

Q: *What about finding my voice?*

A: Voice is what emerges when you stop performing, when your voice on the page flows from your voice off the page, its particular rhythms and vernacular and sensibility. As you reveal more forms of expression, your voice grows more supple. You can be blunt *and* vulnerable, sad *and* funny, erudite *and* vulgar.

Consider a young American writer living in Paris some years ago. He's produced two serious novels and is at work on a third when, one sunny morning, heading to his studio, he notices the water released from the fire hydrants tracing the curbs in iridescent currents. It is, he thinks, "just the sort of thing that makes us loonies cheerful." He resolves, then and there, to allow himself as much freedom of movement as that water.

The result is *The Adventures of Augie March*, whose delirious prose marks the liberation of Saul Bellow from the prison of respectability. At last, the full range of his personality reaches the page, the wise, profane voices he absorbed growing up, the infectious cadences of the four languages spoken in his home. Forget "finding" your voice. It's there already, in the hydrant of your past, awaiting release.

Q: *Is it cool if I check the internet real quick?*

A: Of course. It's your life. But remember: writing is an attention racket. If an open browser is enough to tempt you out of your story, don't expect the reader to stay in it.

Q: *How important is style?*

A: When I hear the word *style*, I see a writer pushing too hard, stepping between the reader and her world. Style is doomed to the exact extent it implies a *conscious effort to shape the language*. Why? Because your artistic unconscious is far more powerful as a creative tool than your conscious mind. Don't throw beautiful words at the page and expect them to amount to truth. Style is the residue produced by a dogged pursuit of truth.

Q: *My writers' group says my story isn't believable, but it really happened!*

A: Not really a question, but I hear this a lot. Chances are your portrayal skimps on character motivation and psychic fallout. There's too much *what happened*, not enough *how* and *why* and *to what end*. Readers may also sense bias—that you've arranged the events in a manner that's too flattering to the writer. Unreliable narrators don't often work in nonfiction.

The contract for fiction is more flexible. Readers will suspend disbelief in exchange for a story in which the character arcs *feel* true. That doesn't mean we can abuse the terms of this contract. Screenwriters get paid to portray morning breath as minty fresh and gunshot wounds as minor inconveniences. You don't.

Plausibility matters even in speculative fiction. Why? Because you have to build an entire imaginary world for the reader, one that is coherent, logical, and internally consistent. That doesn't mean miracles are off the table. A very old man with enormous wings can fall from the sky and land in a small village, as happens in Márquez's eponymous short story. But the villagers must react with a sense of bafflement and wonder that registers as recognizable.

Q: *How do I revise?*

A: Ask the same question of every word: *What work does it do?*
First draft:

Pam walked outside and saw her wife nuzzling the landscaper and her heart chopped like the blurring rotors of a bullet-strafed helicopter sent whirling into the abyss of her bruised, grief-gushing soul.

Second draft:

Pam walked outside and saw her wife nuzzling the landscaper and her heart chopped.

Another way of thinking about this comes from the writer Jim Shepard, who speaks about the *rate of revelation*. When readers receive new and essential info, their rate of revelation is high. When they are given redundant or inessential info—dragged away from the story and into the weeds—their rate of revelation drops and their interest starts to drift.

Q: *Is there any such thing as surefire writing advice?*

A: No. You can and should find an exception to everything I've said. Only a fool speaks with assurance about artistic creation. Take what you can from this book and leave the rest behind. But a few reminders, before I head back to the cave.

Every decision you make matters. It matters that you used the word *anxious* when you meant *eager*. It matters that you chose a comma, and not a semicolon, to separate those independent clauses. It matters that you jumped ship with your heroine on the brink of ruin.

The reader brings her patient heart to your work. She arrives ready to dream your dream. But if you betray her enough times, if you make a habit of lazy, self-regarding decisions, if you fail to grant your characters the love they deserve, she will find another dream.

We are living in an era of screen addiction and capitalist pornography. As a species, we are squandering the exalted gifts of consciousness, losing our capacity to pay attention, to imagine the suffering of others. You are a part of all this. It involves you. This is the hard labor we're trying to perform: convincing strangers to translate our specks of ink into stories capable of generating rescue.

I mentioned before, or maybe I didn't, the ancient feeling I get when I read a beautiful story. It's as if I'm a little kid again and something very sad has happened and it's winter and night has blackened the branches above, I'm very stirred up, close to tears actually, because I can see—I've been *made* to see—the sorrow that everyone is lugging around and the cruel things this sorrow makes them do and still I want to forgive them. I want to forgive every last sorry one of them. God, I love that feeling.

ACKNOWLEDGMENTS

The sort of teaching I do is about a tenth as difficult as your average public school teacher. Those people should be paid a million dollars a year. CEOs should have to beg them for office supplies. With that said, most everything in this book is the result of having been given the opportunity to teach (and therefore think about) writing. Thanks to:

Lee Zacharias at UNC-Greensboro, Rebecca King at the Cambridge Center for Adult Education, Lad Tobin and Elizabeth Graver at Boston College, John Skoyles at Emerson College, Eve Bridburg at Grub Street, Anne Greene at Wesleyan, Ann Marie Lipinski and James Geary at the Nieman Fellowship, Andrea, Mike, and the gang at Denver Lighthouse, Andre Dubus III at UMass-Lowell, all the heroes at Hugo House, Tom DeMarchi at the Sanibel Island Writers Conference, Pam Houston and Karen Nelson at Writing By Writers, Cheryl Strayed at Esalen Writers Camp, Ellen Lesser at the PGWC, Beth Storey at MMW, Susan Tovsky at Orchard Cove, and all the folks who ever invited me to a writing conference, MFA program, college class, or private workshop. I'm grateful to all the students who showed up, in every sense of that phrase.

ACKNOWLEDGMENTS

Shout-outs to the writers who have been my teachers, a list that includes grad school comrades, fellow adjunct rats, and the various superheroes from whom I stole my best material: Paul Salopek, Tom Finkel, John Dufresne, Lynne Barrett, Camille Dungy, Victor Cruz, Mark Smith-Soto, Lisa Breschi, Samantha Dunn, Matthew Zapruder, Rebecca Makkai, Aimee Bender, Lorrie Moore, George Saunders, Jim Shepard, Keith Morris, David Blair. Special thanks to Jenni Ferrari-Adler for believing in me, to Emily Bell for gently compelling me to be a better writer, and the Zando gang for putting books into the world.

To Josephine, Jude, and Irvo: I love you. I am working to learn more about what that means. Thanks for being there each day to teach me. Last (and first) of all, to my brilliant wife, the novelist Erin Almond, without whom this book would not exist.

PERMISSIONS

with the permission of The Permissions Company, LLC on behalf of Copper Canyon Press, coppercanyonpress.org.

Portions of "The Price of Entitlement, the Wisdom of Failure" appeared, in altered form, in *Poets & Writers*, under the titles "The Problem of Entitlement" and "Confessions of a Failed Novelist."

A version of "The Man at the Top of the Stairs" was previously published in *Ploughshares*, Winter 2020–21.

ABOUT THE AUTHOR

STEVE ALMOND is the author of twelve books of fiction and nonfiction, including *All the Secrets of the World* and the *New York Times* bestsellers *Candyfreak* and *Against Football*. His essays and reviews have been published in venues ranging from the *New York Times Magazine* to *Ploughshares* to *Poets & Writers*, and his short fiction has appeared in *Best American Short Stories*, *The Pushcart Prize*, *Best American Mystery Stories*, and *Best American Erotica*. Almond is the recipient of grants from the Massachusetts Cultural Council and the National Endowment for the Arts. He cohosted the *Dear Sugars* podcast with his pal Cheryl Strayed for four years and teaches creative writing at the Nieman Fellowship at Harvard and Wesleyan. He lives in Arlington, Massachusetts, with his family and his anxiety.